WHITE AS COTTON

GARRY HUFF

CITIOFBOOKS, INC.
3736 Eubank NE Suite A1
Albuquerque, NM 87111-3579
www.citiofbooks.com
Hotline: 1 (877) 389-2759
Fax: 1 (505) 930-7244

Ordering Information:
Quantity sales. Special discounts are available on quantity purchases by corporations, associations, and others. For details, contact the publisher at the address above.

Printed in the United States of America.
ISBN-13:   Paperback   979-8-89391-628-7
             eBook   979-8-89391-629-4

Library of Congress Control Number: 2025906999

Jack hadn't noticed how much Cara and Vera looked alike. If they didn't have on different color dresses he couldn't tell them apart. "Master Jack if you and Vera needs me I'll be free after I drop off these towels." said Otis.

Jacks hand was over Vera's shoulder, he was using her for a crush. "No Cara I'm just going down to have a talk to Sam. Dawn should be done with her bath by the time I'm finished." Cara's face took on a hurt look so Jack changed his mind and decided to have Cara find Otis and have him meet him in the office as soon as possible. "Yes, Master Jack." said Cara as her smile returned.

As Jack entered the office, Sam was behind the desk. "Are you feeling better?" Sam asked, as Jack took his arm from around Vera's neck. Sam started going through a large stack of papers even before Jack got to sit down. "From what I figure Carter must have sold off close to twenty slaves in the last few months." Sam told Jack. "Is there any way we can track them?" Jack asked after he got seated. "We can have some posters sent out but it may do no good." Sam said. Sam seemed a bit surprised to see Otis come into the office. "Master Jack, Cara tells me you were looking for me." Otis said as he stood before Jack with his hands behind his back." That's right Otis sit down in that chair and tell me how long you lived here on this plantation." Jack said pointing a finger at the chair across from him. "I'z born here master." said Otis as he took a seat. "Otis is about sixty." Sam said trying to help Otis remember. Otis if I say the name could you tell me what the person looks like?" Jack asked. "I'll do my best." Otis told Jack and Sam. Jack kept the two men in the office for over two hours going over every detail about the missing twenty slaves that Carter must have sold before he was killed.

Just when Jack thought he was finished Otis asked if Dawn had put the slave Maple on the list. All the blood left Sams face when Otis brought up Maples name. "Who is Maple?" asked Jack. "That's enough for tonight." Sam said after the blood returned to his face. Otis you go tell the cook to put dinner on the table, then go tell Miss Dawn that dinner will be early." Sam told Otis as he walked him to the door. Sam closed the door behind Otis he walked into the hallway. Sam could feel Jacks eyes on him even before he turned around to face him. "Who is Maple?" Jack asked again. Sam sat down in his high-backed chair and set in silence before speaking. "Maple is my daughter by a slave by the name Easter."

"Easter is also the mother of the boy that brought you home with Dawn?" "Is Easter Vera and Caras mother too?" Jack asks as he sits up in his set. Sam shook his head before speaking. "Yes, she is all their mother."

"What made you about to have a heart attack when you heard Maples name?" asked Jack.

"Where would be the best place to start?" Sam asked as he wiped the sweat from his forehead. "When I was fifteen my pa brought Easter to the house and told me, this is your bed wench from now on."

Jack sat back in his seat because he could tell this was going to take some time.

"Pa had brought Easter back from New Orleans to me here because she was so light skinned. It was his idea to bread niggers so light skinned they could pass as white folk." Sam paused for a moment to see what Jacks reaction was going to be before he went on. "Well it didn't take Easter long to get pregnant and she was only fifteen when she had Maple. As soon as the baby was weaned, Pa took Maple and put her with nanny. We never saw maple again until twenty years ago."

"Okay what does this got to do with where she is now?" Jack asked with anger in his voice.

"I'm getting to that Jack just give me a minute."

"Go on." Jack said.

"I don't know if you've been told but each year we have a spring deflowering." said Sam.

"A what?" asked Jack.

"Each year we gather up all the virgins and break them in over the weekend." said Sam.

"In other words, you used them like cattle." said Jack.

"Yes." Sam said." Well over the weekend that Maple came of age she was added to the virgin girls and without knowing it Maple got pregnant. Easter became pregnant with Cotton and Mary became pregnant with Dawn. Mary had forced Easter out of the house and when she found out about Maples child she went nuts. She found out where Maple was staying and she rode out there and shot Maple and the unborn child. Me and Carter met her on the way back and we got into a big fight right there in the creek bed. Mary's horse through her and her head hit a rock killing her. Two years later Easter had the twins and then she died."

"Then Cotton is Cara and Vera's blood brother?" asked Jack.

"Yes." Was all Sam would say.

Dawn had finished her bath and collected Vera and Cara up to help her get ready for the afternoon's activities. Otis tapped lightly on the door before calling Dawns name. Let him in he heard a voice say from the other side. Vera opened the door then stepped back so Otis could come in.

"Miss Dawn, Master Sam says to tell you that supper will be early tonight."

"Thank you Otis I'll be down in just a few more minutes." Dawn told Otis as he turned to. Otis stopped and turned around in the hallway. "Master Jack is looking to find out what happened to Maple." Otis told Dawn. "How did he find out about her Otis?" Dawn asked. Both Dawn and Otis turned to face Vera. "The boy by the name of Cotton is the only one he asked me about." Vera told Dawn. "You can go now Otis, I'll find out who told Jack at dinner. I must get dressed." Dawn said as she walked to her closet and took out a black dress that would show off her cleavage. "OH miss Dawn you look so pretty in that dress." Cara said as Dawn stood in front of the mirror.

Jack and Sam were already seated when Dawn come into the dining room. Otis pulled out Dawns chair for her then walked over and stood by the door after Dawn was seated. "It's good to see you back on your feet Jack." Dawn told Jack as she undid her napkin and placed it on her lap.

"It's good to be out of that room even if it's just for a little while." Jack said with a smile.

Jacks going to help me track down those slaves Carter sold." Sam said with a mouth full of food.

"You should not talk with your mouth full." Dawn scolded. Dawn turned her attention to Jack after Sam went on eating as if he hadn't heard her." Jack Otis was telling me your looking for a slave by the name of Maple. Is that true?"

Sam started chocking and Otis ran to him to try to help.

"Are you going to be alright?" Dawn asked. Sam shook his head yes but he was still choking as he rose from the table. "Otis you help me to my room and you two enjoy your dinner." Sam said as he left the room.

Dawn and Jack were left alone once Sam and Otis had gone. "well did you find her?" Dawn asked.

"Yes I found out all about her." Jack said then put a bit of food in his mouth so he could drop the subject.

"Vera is so excited about having a big sister." Dawn said trying to get Jack talking about Maple again.

"I'm afraid she's going to be disappointed about Maple, she's dead." Jack said with no sign of emotion. Dawn didn't know why but it hurt her to think that Vera was in for another disappointment." Vera will just have to accept that Cara and Cotton are her only kin." Jack said as he stared at the rise and fall of Dawn's breast with his blue eyes.

Dawn felt like she was sitting there without a stitch of clothing. His eyes seemed to take on a hunger that she put there. It was exciting and frightening at the same time. Dawn was torn between seeing just how far she could take this or acting like a southern lady and gently call Jack on his hungry stair. The decision was made for her when Jack pushed back his chair and rose from the table. "Miss Dawn I hate leaving a good-looking lady sitting alone but my shoulder is beginning to hurt and the thought of you seeing me cry is unbearable."

"That's a shame." said Dawn. "There is nothing melts a woman's heart like a boy crying."

A little laugh escaped Jack's mouth as he turned to leave Dawn sitting by herself. Jack decided that he had enough trouble in his life and Dawn had trouble written all over her. He had to admit her planned almost worked. Jack was a long way into her web before he caught himself. He had come to far to turn back now. Sam Sarrows had so many offspring that Sam didn't know that the man named Jack Benson was one of them.

Thirty-one years ago, Sam had Jacks mother from the field and used her as a bed wench. Jack and his mother both were sold to a hotel owner in New Orleans. Jack was set free upon the death of his master. Not only was he set free but the Whore house and the gambling house were left to him. Jack couldn't believe his luck when he found out that Sam Sarrows was in his place. Now here he was standing in the house that once belonged to Sam. Jack smiled as he thought of Dawn throwing herself at him. The smile left his face as he thought of using his half-sister like that. Jacks determination to get back at Sam for making his mother's life a pure hell. For that Sam Sarrows had to pay.

Vera was in Jacks room when he entered it. Vera had taken off her dress and climbed into the bath water Dawn had left. "I'ze sorry Master Jack I was just washing off." Vera said as she rose to get out of the tub.

"Go ahead and take your bath." Jack said as he laid down on his bed looking at the smiling girl playing in the water. That's your half-sister too Jack told himself as he turned his head to look at the ceiling.

Dawn wasn't sure whether or not to be mad at Jack or to respect him for being a gentleman. "How did it go Miss Dawn; did he ask you to marry up with him?" Cara asked. "Where is Vera?" Dawn asked without answering Cara's question. "She's in Master Jack's room I think." Cara said. Dawn had told herself that she wasn't going to be jealous of Jack and Vera but she had put on her sexiest dress and Jack had left her sitting alone. "Damn." Dawn said with a stomp of her foot then began taking off her dress. After she had gotten the dress off she pitched it to the floor. "Take off that dress Cara." Dawn ordered. "Do what Miss Dawn?" Cara asked not sure if she had heard Dawn right the first time. "I said take-off that dress." Cara protested all the time she was removing her dress. "Now put that on." Dawn ordered pointing toward the black dress laying on the floor.

Jack was amazed at how unbothered Vera was about her nudity. He was going to have to have her sent back to her sisters before he forgets who she is. "Vera." Jack said still looking at the ceiling. "Yes, Master Jack." Vera said before he could finish his words. Jack could hear the sounds that told him that Vera was getting out of the tub. Jack didn't turn his head until he felt Vera standing by the bed. "Vera, I want you to gather your things and go back to the room you share with your sister." "Oh, Master Jack I'm sorry for taking that bath." Vera said pointing toward the tub like she had stolen something valuable. "That has nothing to do with it Vera." Jack said as he raised up to look at her.

"Tell Vera what it is and I won't do it no more. I promise Master Jack."

"Vera you have done nothing wrong it's just that I want my room to myself." Jack said.

Vera's dark eyes stared at Jack before she spoke. "Master Jack, if you be needing a bed wench, I." the words froze in her throat.

"Vera I'll chose my own bed wench, is that understood!" Jack roared not cutting the sharpness from his voice.

"Yes, Master Jack Vera understands." Vera said as she hung her head.

Jack pointed toward the door "Get your things and get out."

No matter how hard she tried Vera couldn't hold back her tears as she hastily gathered her few belongings and left. As soon as Vera was gone Jack collapsed on the bed. Jack felt something on his cheek and reached up and touched it. "What is this?" Jack asked himself as he felt the wetness. Jack had let his hate for Sam rule him for so long that he didn't remember ever crying over anyone but his mother. Making Vera leave had to be done. Jack knew that he could control his sexual feelings just so for then the beast that really drove a man gets in charge. Should he tell them that he's their brother.

Dawn was getting ready to yell at Vera when she noticed that Vera was already crying and carrying her few things. "What is the matter with you." Dawn asked as she took ahold of Vera's arm. "Master Jack told me to leave, I think he is going to move a bed wench in there,

Miss Dawn." Vera said seeing an ally instead of a rival. "What can we do Miss Dawn he the master we got to do as he says."

"You might have to do what Master Jack says but I don't." Dawn couldn't understand the smile her words brought to Vera's face. Dawn's anger had blinded her to the fact that she was as powerless as Vera. Dawn remembered that the last time she had tried to use her sexual charms on Jack, he threw them back in her face. The thought of that happening again was out of the question. There must be a way to reach Jack and if there was a kink in his armor she was going to find it. "Cara, you help your sister take her things to your room."

Dawns hand shook a little as she started to knock on Jacks door. "Come in." came a voice on the other side. "Oh, it's you." Jack said as he set up when Dawn came through the door. The fake smile left Dawn's face even before the door closed. "Mr. Benson, I do not know what kind of whore house you lived in in New Orleans but you'll not turn my home into one." Dawn yelled. Dawn's eyes widened in fear as she saw the anger consume Jack.

"Woman, what are you talking about? I have no intention of turning my house into a whore house." Jack was saying as he advanced on Dawn. For every step he took towards her Dawn took one back until she was against the door.

"Vera told me all about it." said Dawn.

"About what?" Jack asked.

"About how you were going to bring in a field hand in here for a bed wench." Dawn replied.

"Vera offered to be my bed wench but I through her out just as I'm doing to you." Jack said as he stepped back so Dawn could get the door open.

Dawn was literally shaking when she reached her room. Dawn walked over and stood in front of the full length mirror. What is it about me that makes him so angry when he's around me, she asked herself as she looked in the mirror. There was no reason for Jack to treat her like just another white slave. Come to think of it he treats Vera better than he does me. Dawn said as she walked to the bed.

"Vera does you think Master Jack is going to sell us off?" Cara asked. "He was pretty angry but I don't think he will put us on the auction block." said Vera. "This is the only place that I've called home and I would just die if we were sold to someone who took you away." Cara said between sobs. Vera put her arms around her sister. "We will stay together always even if we got to run away to do it." Vera said. "Oh no Vera we can't run, you know what them slave catchers does to us if they catch us. We must stay here no matter what we's got to do we must stay here." Cara said.

Jack had to get out of his room if one of the girls came offering to be his bed wench again he was going to get one to keep them quiet. There was none in the hallway as Jack stepped out and closed the door behind him. Otiss was headed to his room when Jack met him at the foot of the stairs. "Master Jack is there something Otiss can do for you before I go to bed?" Otiss asked.

"Yes Otiss there is." Jack said.

"You just tell Otiss what you want and I'll do it for you Master Jack." Otis said with a smile.

"I want you to show me where the young slave girls are that want to be my bed wench stay." It was the first time he'd heard Otiss laugh out loud. "Sure enough Master Jack. I'll show you the best bed wenches on the place is." Otiss said as he lead Jack out of the front door.

Jack followed Otiss to a long house set apart from the other slave quarters. Most of the slave girls were already in their beds when Otiss and Jack came into the house. "These girls was put here by Master Sam for breeding." Otiss said as he lit a lamp by the door. Beds lined both walls and the young ladies that sat up in them were of all different ages. "It's him." Jack heard one of them say. Some of the girls lay nude in the summer night heat. Some of the girls hastily grabbed dresses to put on.

"Master is there any of these that you want?" Otiss asked.

Jacks blue eyes scanned through the dim light looking for what he thought would put a stop to Dawn's and Vera's meddling. "Master is I'm what you're looking for?" a weak voice called from the darkness. The voice had come from behind him and as Jack turned around the light from the lamp shown upon a light skinned girl of about seventeen. She stood five foot five and weighed 110 lbs. Her long black hair hung past her hips. "This here is Sarah, Master Jack, she has been here for three years." Otiss told Jack.

"With a bath and a new dress, I think you will do just fine." said Jack. "Get your dress and follow me."

Sam had bought Sarah three years ago and used her for a bed wench for some time before he went to another. Sarah had never been to the big house before because Sam didn't want her in the house around Dawn. Jack couldn't help but laugh as he watched Sarah look the house over like she was in heaven. "This way." Jack said as he lead the way up the stairs. Sarah stopped as Jack entered his room. She stood and stared at the room from the hallway like it was a cage. "You can come in, you don't have to stay out there." Jack said. Slowly Sarah entered the room and while Jack lit the lamp his back was to Sarah. As he turned around Sarah had taken off the dirty dress and dropped it on the floor. The pallet that Otiss had fixed for Vera was still on the floor by the tub. Jack stopped Sarah as she started walking to his bed. "No." Jack said. "You get in that tub then you go to sleep on that pallet." He told her. Sarah walked over to the tub of cold water and put her foot in it. "Oh!" Sarah cried as she lowered herself into the cold water. Jack could tell that Sarah had never taken a bath in a tub before. Once her body got use to the cold water she was like a child in a swimming hole. The dirt slowly came off Sarah and her long bluish black hair hung below her hips and water dripped from its long stands.

"Master, am I clean enough for you?" Sarah asked as she stepped from the tub. "Yes, Sarah you look much better now." Jack said as he took off his shirt. Sarah hadn't noticed the wound on his shoulder until now. "Your hurt Master." "Yes Sarah, I've been hurt but it's getting better." "You just lay down and I'll get on top so you won't hurt your arm anymore." Sarah said. "I know you thought you were brought here for my pleasure but all I want you to do tonight is go over there and go to sleep." Jack told her. Sarah was puzzled by Jack but he is the Master that took her out of the whore house, that's what the others called it.

Jack was awake when Otiss knocked on the door the next morning. He was laying on his bed looking at Sarah who laid on her pallet just as nude as when she had gotten out of the tub. The dirty flock dress was still on the floor where she had tossed it. Sarah watched Jack as he got dressed and her eye's kept drifting back to the dress on the floor. Jack watched Sarah as she slowly rose to her feet and walked over to pick up the dirty dress on the floor.

"Don't put that back on." Jack told her. Sarah was confused, surely Master didn't expect her to walk around with no dress on. "You stay here, I'll be back soon." Jack said as he left the room and closed the door behind him.

Sarah was worried she had made a mistake, at least at the whore house she could wear a dirty dress and go outside. Sarah thought that the new Master was handsome enough, but it bothered her that he hadn't made love to her even after she had bathed. "These white men sure are a strange lot." she said in a low voice.

Cara opened the door when Jack knocked on it. "Well Master Jack you are up early this morning." Dawn said with a laugh. A blank look came to Dawn's face replacing her smile when Jack asked for a dress. "This may sound crazy but I need one of your dresses." Jack said. Both Cara and Vera started to laugh but quickly stopped themselves. Dawn wasn't a bit amused. "What do you need one of my dresses for Mr. Benson?" Dawn asked emphasizing Mr.

"I took your advice and brought in a bed wench." He told her. "You what, my advice, I never told you to do such a thing!" Dawn yelled. "I only need to borrow one until I get to town." Jack went on to say. Dawn almost fell back on her bed not believing what she was hearing. "Do you want me to pick one out Miss Dawn?" Cara asked. "Yes, for God's sake, get him one or he will have the who-." Dawn started to say then changed to "bed wench running through the house buck ass naked." "No not that one." Dawn would say every time Cara pulled one out of the closet. Dawn finally settled on a yellow dress with white dots and Jack could tell she was hurting on the inside.

Sarah was sitting on the pallet brushing her hair when Jack came in carrying the dress. "Oh, Master that's so pretty." She said as she threw the brush down and jumped to her feet. "Put this on and follow me." Jack instructed as he handed the dress to Sarah.

As Jack and Sarah stepped out into the hall he noticed Vera and Cara peeking out the door. Once they knew Jack had seen them the two girls quickly ran and set on the bed. They had been in such a hurry that they had forgot to close the door. "You two come out here." Jack ordered. Both girls came out with their heads hung low. "Sarah these two peepers are Cara and Vera. They will show you where to eat and how to clean my room, won't you." Jack said. "Yes, Master Jack." Both girls answered at the same time. "I'm going to get something to eat because I think I'm going to have a long day." Said Jack.

Dawn expected to see Jack and his bed wench setting at the table when she entered the dining room but the only one's there was Otis and Sam. "Pa do you know what that man has done?" Dawn asked as she sat down. "What has he done this time?" Sam asked a little annoyed at Dawn's persistent bitching. "He's done brought a whore into this house and he must have brought her here with no cloths because he borrowed a dress from me for her to wear." Said Dawn.

"Now Dawn you were mad at him yesterday because you thought he was going to use Vera for a bed wench. Now your mad because he didn't. Now you got to understand that we are here just because he is letting us stay in his house." Sam shouted.

Dawn was about to shout back but Jack entering the room stopped her. "Well if it aint Master Jack the plantation pimp." Dawn said sarcastically.

Her words like a slap in the face that took the smile from Jacks face.

"Jack I must apologize for my daughters tongue it's the sharpest part of her." Sam said trying to smooth over the anger he saw in Jack's eyes. "Dawn's just not use to having a bed wench in the house is all." Jack was talking to Sam but his eyes were on Dawn. "You can leave this whore house anytime you like Sam and take your ungrateful daughter with you." Jack shot back.

"There's no need to turn us out in the cold." Sam pleaded. "I will see that Dawn keeps her mouth shut Jack. Just don't make us leave."

Dawn thought she had gone too far and she knew that her pa was right. This man could put both of them out on the road anytime he wanted. "Jack I'm sorry. I don't know what comes over me but I promise that I'll keep my feelings to myself from now on." Dawn said.

"See that you do." Jack said angrily, then turned to Otis. "Otis go get Sarah and bring her Cara and Vera here right now." Jack told him.

Dawn was about to protest but Sam pointed a finger at her.

"Yes Master." Otis said with a shocked look on his face. Sarah was getting acquainted with Cara and Vera when Otis knocked on the door that was open. The three of them couldn't help but notice the strange look on Otis's face. "What is it Otis?" Vera asked.

"Master Jack just had a big fight with Miss Dawn and he sent me to fetch you three and bring you to the dining room." said Otis. "Did Master Jack say what he wanted with us?" Vera asked. No Otis said by shaking his head, "He said right now."

The three girls had nothing but doom going through their heads as they slowly walked down stairs. The only slaves that were allowed in the dining room kitchen servants and Otis. The fear only grew stronger as Otis told how Master Jack was about to put Master Sam and Miss Dawn out of the house. "I've never seen him so mad." Otis kept saying as he ushered the three girls toward the dining room. Vera looked at Jack setting at the head of the table and then to Dawn and Sam for a clue of what this is about. But didn't find one in any of them. Vera was surprised when Sarah asked, "Have we done something to upset you?" They were all surprised to see a smile come to Jacks face.

"No Sarah you have done nothing wrong. I just wanted to set here and have you, Vera and Cara join me and the rest of us for breakfast." Jack replied. Every mouth in the room dropped open in shock. Every eye in the room was on Jack like he had suddenly lost his mind. Dawn started to protest but one look from Jack stopped her. Sam wanted to protest as bad as Dawn but thought he had better not push his luck.

"Sit." Jack said gave a hand jester for the three, "and you Otis sit beside Sam." Sarah was the only one to quickly accept the New Master's strange new ways of doing things and started filling her plate with food. Jack waited until everyone had food in front of them before he spoke again. "Isn't this nice we're all sitting here like a big happy family." Sam started choking and Jack didn't know if it were his words or the food that caused it.

Sarah was the only one who didn't sit in silence besides Jack. "I shour didn't know that house slaves had it so good." she said with a giggle. "Believe me, it wasn't like this when I owned this place." Sam said with discussed in his voice.

"Now Sam, we all know how you gambled away everything. While you set at a poker table your over seer sold fifty slaves and you didn't even know it." Jack shot back. "If you'll excuse me I've got work to do." Sam said as he rose from the table. "Otis when you're finished. I'll need your help in my office." Sam said before he left.

"I've had all I can stand for one morning." Dawn said as she rose. "Vera you and Cara come with me." Dawn said. "No Dawn, they will be helping Sarah clean this whole house. From now on, you will treat them like a sister not a slave." Jack told her.

"Well who's going to do my hair and clean my room?" Dawn questioned. "You are Miss Dawn or it won't get done." Jack replied. "Master Jack, you don't want Vera and me to do what Miss Dawn say's no more." Cara asked. "From now on you are to treat her like a sister and not your master, is that understood?" asked Jack. "Yes, Master Jack." both Vera and Cara said at the same time.

Dawn stomped her foot and left cursing Jack the whole time she was walking.

"Start your cleaning here." Jack told them as he rose to leave. "Miss Dawn must have done something bad to make Master Jack so mad at her." Vera said as she started cleaning the table. "I wish I knew what that was, I wouldn't wan't Master Jack that mad at me." Sarah told them as she stacked the plates into one stack. "I bet Miss Dawn is in her room crying her eyes out." Cara told them as she looked towards the hallway.

"You heard Master Jack. We got to do as he says." Vera told her sister. "I can't wait until tonight." Sarah said as she looked at Vera. "What's so special about tonight." Vera asked. "I'm going to give him so much loven that he will want to keep me here in the big house forever." Sarah replied. "You didn't do it with him last night?" Vera asked. "No and that was so strange to even after I took a bath and all." Sarah said. "Well don't feel bad. I offered him me and Miss Dawn tried to but we done no good." Vera said.

"Maybe he just don't like women." Cara said feeling left out of the talk. "You mean he likes boys?" Sarah asked. Vera and Cara looked at each other puzzled as to what Sarah was talking about. 233"Of course that don't make since either. Because if he liked boys he would of brought one in here and not me." Sarah was saying more to herself then to the others.

Sam set in his office trying to think of a way to get rid of Jack besides killing him. "The only way I'm going to get my place back before Jack gives it all away is to set up an accident." Like he had done to his late wife. Killing Jack wouldn't be as easy as it had been with Mary, she didn't pack a gun. Sam thought a few minutes and a smile came to his face as he saw Otis enter the room. "Otis go out and find Cotton and tell him to saddle three horses and wait for me and Master Jack out front." Sam told Otis. "Yes Master Sam. I'll go do that right now." Otis said as he left.

Cara was right. Dawn was sitting in her room crying her eyes out. Jack Benson hadn't been in her life for more then a week and had made her a slave just like Cara and Vera. He had taken what was to be the happiest days of her life and turned them into a living hell. What made it so bad was she was still in love with him. If it wasn't for that little detail she would pack her bags and leave Master Jack to his bed wenches. She had noticed how made her pa got this morning. He was more than likely downstairs packing his bags right now. If Jack wanted a bed wench, Dawn decided she would become the one that lived in his room. How to get rid of Sarah was going to be hard to do and make Jack think it was his idea.

Dawn striped off her dress and dug through her closet until she found the dress that looked like one Vera and Cara might wear and put it on. The three girls were just finishing up the dining room when Dawn came in.

"Miss Dawn is there something I can do for you?" Cara asked. "No, I've not come to get you. I've come to help you clean." Dawn said. "Miss Dawn I don't think Master Jack ment for you to act like, like us." Vera said

"I know what Master Jack said and I'm going to treat you like a sister. If that means working along beside you, then I will." Dawn said.

"Well Miss Dawn we have about finished here. So we can start on Master Jacks bedroom." Sarah said as she started towards the stairs. "does Master Jack know you're doing this?" Cara asked as they went up the stairs. "You let me worry about Jack and what he will think of me." Dawn said. Vera thought Miss Dawn had lost her mind but wasn't about to say anything. Dawn was kinda curious as what Jack would do when he saw her with the other girls. He would either laugh or put her in a mental hospital, she thought. As they approached Jacks door Dawns stomach started churning. "Master Jack we are here to clean your room." Sarah said as she opened the door. To Dawns relief there was no one in there.

Otis had come and told Jack that Sam needed him in the office because he had found a way to find where Carter had sold the slaves. Sam was all smiles when Jack entered the office. "What's this all about?" Jack asked. "I think I can find where Carter sold the slaves. If he kept any records they would be at his house. So we just go there and find any paper's he kept. Sam said. It sounded like a waste of time to Jack but Carter might be stupid enough to put down on paper who he sold the slaves to.

"Okay Sam, I'll get my guns and you have my horse saddled. "Jack said. "I've already had that done. They are out front waiting." Sam told Jack. "I'll be right back." Jack told Sam, as he started up the stairs to his room to get his guns. Because Jack had the feeling he was going to need them before the day is through.

Cotton stood holding the three horses out in front of the house, thinking the new master was the one who had sent for him. The last time Cotton had seen the new master, he was lying in a wagon bleeding to death. If it hadn't been for the new master and Miss Dawn he would probably be in the cane field being worked to death. Otis had said nothing about who the horses were for but Cotton didn't really care. He just wished whoever they were for would hurry up and come get them, he was getting hot out in the sun.

The girls were hard at work cleaning Jacks room when he came in. He wasn't surprised to see Vera, Cara and Sarah there but he couldn't tell who the one that was bent over the tub dipping water out was because the only part of that he could see was her ass. Sarah was the first to see Master Jack come in. "Master is we doing a good job?" she asked as she tucked in the clean sheet she had just put on the bed.

"Yes Sarah, you all are doing a good job." Jack told her not taking his eyes off the one at the tub. "Vera who is your friend?" Jack asked as he walked over to where Dawn tried to keep her backside to him. Dawn couldn't believe the look on Jacks face when she turned to look at him.

"Dawn what do you think your doing in that get up, working like a slave?"

"Well Master Jack I thought as you want to treat me like one of your niggers, I would dress and act the part." Dawn said sarcastically.

"Master Jack it was all her idea." Vera said. The whole room turned to Vera because she had said her instead of Miss Dawn. Until they all started staring at her Vera didn't realize what she had done. "I'ze sorry Miss Dawn I just wasn't thinking."

"It's ok Vera. Master Jack has gotten what he wanted. You are thinking like he wanted." Jack looked at Dawn and started to say that she was wrong. But the more he thought about it, he knew she was right.

"Dawn you can play house maid if you like, I've got more important things to do right now." Jack put on his gun belt and cupped the Winchester in his good arm and walked out shaking his head.

"At least Master Jack didn't shoot you." Sarah said with a laugh. The smile left her face just about as fast as it had come on it when she seen that Miss Dawn wasn't the least bit amused by the look Dawn was giving her.

Cotton was glad to see the front door open but thought it strange that only two people came out of the house.

"Why is there three horses?" Jack asked when he saw them. "I thought we could take Cotton with us and he could hunt for…" "Can he read?" Jack asked before Sam could finish.

"No but he can check the out buildings and if he found anything he can bring it to us." Sam said. Jack thought that it was a stupid idea but if Sam wanted to try it then what could it hurt.

"Glad to see you back on your feet Master Jack." Cotton said as Sam and Jack reached him.

"Get on that horse." Sam said after Cotton didn't say anything to him. Cotton looked at Jack to make sure he wanted him too."

Go ahead." Jack said as he mounted his horse. "Yes Master." Cotton climbed up then let Sam and Jack lead the way, because he had no idea where they were going or what they were going to do.

Sam lead the way to Carters place. While Cotton followed just enjoying the ride. Jack slowed his horse until Cotton caught up. "They tell me your Cara and Vera's brother." Jack said to Cotton when he caught up. "Yes Master. I'm the only kin they have here."

Jack riding along talking to Cotton was making Sam very nervous. Had Jack figured out his plan. Sam wondered. The overseers house came into view so Sam motioned for Jack and Cotton to hurry up. Sam was already off his horse by the time Jack and Cotton reached the house.

"You know Sam, It's a shame to let this place go to waste. I think I'll let one of the overseers that has a big family move in here after we search it." Jack said.

"That's a good idea. I have a good man in mind." Sam said as he went up the steps.

"Who do you think is the best man to take over as the head overseer?" Jack asked as he followed Sam up the steps.

"Butch Harder would be my choice." Sam said.

"He's the one that told me about Carter and the five slaves, wasn't he?" Jack asked. "Yes." Sam said as they went through the door. Sam turned to Cotton, "You look in them out buildings for any kind of papers and if you find any, bring them to us." Sam told Cotton. "I'll check the bedroom, and you can start here." Sam told Jack.

Sarah was glad that Dawn had decided to give up the idea of becoming one of the girls. Vera and Cara and Sarah had finished cleaning Jacks room by themselves "Where to next?" Sarah asked as they stepped out into the hallway. "What about Dawns room?" Cara said

"Miss Dawn didn't look like she wanted us around her." Sarah said trying to get the other two to go someplace other than Dawns room. "I think all the men have gone for a while so we can go to our room for a break." Vera told Cara. "That's okay with me." Sarah said. the three girls went as fast as they could to Vera's room.

Dawn sat in her room wondering where the three girls were now. Just so she wouldn't be alone Dawn thought of going back to work just to have someone to talk to. She thought of having Cotton saddle up her horse so she could go for a ride. After sitting alone a few more minutes, Dawn left her room to find the others and see where Jack had gone to in such a hurry.

Cotton only found building that had anything in it but there was no paper of any kind in it. Jack on the other hand found a small room that was filled with papers. The trouble was that there was not one that was in any kind of order.

Sam looked around the bedroom just in case Jack was watching. Seeing that Jack was nowhere in sight. Sam took out a small Dillinger from his pocket and opened it to make sure it was loaded. For his plan to work, he would call for Cotton to come in and when he did he would shoot Jack in the back. Take Jacks gun and shoot Cotton. Sam could say that Cotton shot Jack and he shot Cotton with Jacks gun. After Jack had been buried. Sam would take the forged papers to the right people and he would have his plantation back. "I think this is going to work." Sam said as he closed up the Dillinger. Sam turned to go find Jack, then call Cotton to come in.

Dawn had found Otis and found out that the men had gone to Carters house to look for some kind of papers. She found it strange that Sam had took Cotton with them knowing Cotton couldn't read. and her pa didn't like being around Cotton. Dawn had the blacksmith saddle a horse for her. Then she rode out to see if she could help. Cotton was climbing the steps as Dawn rode up.

"Cotton where's pa and Jack?" She asked even before she got off the horse.

"Their inside." Cotton called back. "Master Sam just called for me." Cotton said as he waited for Dawn at the top of the steps. Just as Dawn reached the door a shot rang out. "What the hell." Dawn said as she rushed through the door. She no sooner stepped through the door then a second shot knocked her back through the air and she hit the ground. "Oh my God!" Sam said as he saw what he had just done. The bullet had hit Jack in the shoulder that had already been hit with the buckshot.

Jack had played dead because he didn't know what kind of a gun he'd been shot by. Jack then remembered a gun laying on the desk with the papers he had been looking through. When he heard a second shot he opened his eyes to see Sam with his back to him. Thinking Sam had shot Cotton too. Jack got the gun off the desk and shot Sam in the back twice before Sam hit the floor. Cotton didn't know who was doing all the shooting or why. Was the new master gone crazy and killing everyone. He just didn't know. Should he go help Miss Dawn or run he asked himself as Jack came out the door carrying a gun.

"Oh please Master don't shoot me." Cotton begged. "I'm not going to shoot you Cotton. I've been shot again myself." Jack said before he saw Dawn laying on the ground. Jack staggered until he was at Dawns side and Cotton dropped to his knees beside him. "Is she dead?" Cotton asked. "No, but she will be if we don't get her some help." Jack told Cotton.

"You go get someone to bring a wagon and send for a doctor. While I stay with her." Jack told Cotton. "Yes Master Jack. I'll go as fast as I can." Jack could tell by the way he was getting light headed that he was losing to much blood to stay continues for long. Before Cotton left Jack had him move Dawn to the shade. She had been shot in her left breast close to her heart.

Dawn opened her eyes and saw Jack sitting beside her. "Why Jack? Why did pa shoot me?" Dawn asked. "It was meant for Cotton not you." Jack told her. Jacks words seemed to confuse her even more. "Don't talk." Jack said when she started to ask another question. It seemed like hours instead of minutes before Cotton, Otis and Vera came with the wagon.

Otis had sent one of the slaves to get the doctor. and bring him to the house as fast as he could. Otis and Cotton put Jack and Dawn in the back of the wagon and run the team of horses as fast as they could for home. Between the two of them the wagon was covered in blood. Vera got sick at first but soon got herself under control and did the best she could to help them.

Otis and Cotton put Dawn and Jack in the same bed until the doctor had come to stop the bleeding. Doctor Fox decided Dawn was in more danger then Jack so he went to work on her while Otis held pressure on Jacks bullet wound to stop him from bleeding to death. Doctor Fox had Vera take off Dawns clothes so he could see how the bullet had gone once it hit her in the breast. Cotton did the same to Jack.

Vera thought of how Dawn would have reacted if she knew that when she first got naked with with Jack, there was four people watching. It was two in the morning before the doctor had them both sleeping and the bleeding stopped. "Can we move Miss Dawn or Jack to another bed?" Vera asked the doctor.

"No not yet. I'm afraid that if we move one of them it would cause one to start bleeding again. They both have lost to much blood already." Doctor Fox said.

Dawn laid on her back and Jack on his front. Cotton, Cara and Otis sat in the hallway just outside the door of Jacks room. Cotton and Cara just stared at one another for a long time before Cara finally asked him "Are you really my brother?"

Cotton studied her for a long time before he answered her as he remembered how Vera had took it when he told her about being her brother. "Yes sister, I am your brother, our mother and pa are the same." He said. Cotton was surprised when Cara took his blood-stained hand in hers and a smile came to her face. "Why did Master Sam try to kill Master Jack and Miss Dawn, Otis?" Cara asked. "I don't know Cara. He must have just gone out of his mind." Otis told her.

Sarah had put up a fight with Otis when he took her back to the so-called whore house. "Master Jack won't be needing a bed wench for a while." He had told her but she didn't want to go back anyway. Otis thought he would have to make Cotton pick Sarah up and pack her out but she went cussing all the way to the whore house. Cara jumped up when Doctor Fox came out of the room into the hallway.

"Is they dead?" She asked.

"No but they're not out of the woods yet." He said.

"Is there anything I can do?" Cara asked.

"Yes there is. You all can go to bed so you will be more help tomorrow." Doctor Fox said.

"That sounds like a good idea." Otis said as he got to his feet. "I'll just sleep here." Cotton said as he stayed seated.

"You will go to bed like the rest of us." Otis told him. "I don't have a bed in the house." Cotton said. Otis reached out a hand to help Cotton to his feet. "You can sleep in that room there." He said pointing to a door down the hall. "I'm going to check on them two and I'll bring you some water for your wash basin." Otis said. "Thank you, Otis." Cotton said as he stuck out his bloody hand for Otis to shake.

Otis shook Cottons hand then went into the room Dawn and Jack laid together in. Vera sat on the pallet by the bath tub. "They don't look to be in any pain." Otis said as he walked over to the bed.

"I think Old Doc. Fox gave them something to help them sleep." Vera said as she came to the bed beside Otis. "If you're going to stay in here with them I'll have a bed put in here for you tomorrow." said Otis. "That would be fine. Thank you, Otis." Vera said. Otis was starting to like the feel of power that he now had until Master Jack got better.

Cotton took a bath in the water Otis had brought to him. Then he took his hand and pushed down on the soft feather mattress on the bed. It sure was a lot softer then the straw bed he was use to sleeping on. After he laid down on it he stared at the ceiling and wondered how long how long he would get to enjoy living in the big house. "With Master Sam gone and the way he got along with Master Jack it could be a long time." He said in a low voice. The softness of the feather bed seemed to envelope him, and in just a few minutes he was sound asleep.

Vera was awakened the next morning by the sound of Dawn crying out in pain. "Miss Dawn you just lie still until I get the doctor. He will give you something for the pain." Vera said. Dawns cry woke Jack from his sleep and he turned onto his side to see who was in bed with him. The pain he felt brought back the memory of what happened yesterday.

Dawn smiled at Jack until she realized that she didn't have any clothes on. "What are you doing here?" She yelled as she pulled the sheet up to her neck. "I thought I'd died and gone to heaven." Jack said.

Vera and the doctor came in as Jack was trying to get out of bed. Jack got as far as putting his feet over the side before he fell back onto Dawn. "Here young man. You just lie back down before you hurt somebody." Doctor Fox told him.

"Vera go get Otis and Cotton to help me." Jack said. "Yes, Master Jack. I'll fetch Cotton he's right down the hall." Vera had no sooner gotten into the hallway when Cotton met her. "Master Jack wants you to help him get out of bed." Vera told him. "You may need Otis too." She added.

"I won't need no help." Cotton said. "I can pack him myself." Cotton went into the room and went straight to the bed. "Master Jack where do you want me to pack you?" Jack hadn't really thought of that after all he was already in his room.

"I would like to go to my own room." Dawn said to the doctor. Jack waited to see what the doctor said before he said anymore to Cotton. "Well okay. If you think you can make it." the doc said. "Cotton you pack Miss Dawn to her room and Vera you go turn down her bed and find Cara. She can stay with Miss Dawn in her room." Otis said from the doorway.

No one knew that Otis was around until he spoke. Jack looked to see who giving orders and a smile came to his face when he saw Otis. Cotton picked Dawn up in his arms as easily as a sack of corn and keeping the sheet tight around her. Vera hurried ahead so the bed would be ready when they reached it.

Cara was already in Dawns room when she got there. "Otis said for you to stay with Miss Dawn and I'm to stay with Master Jack." Vera told Cara as she turned down the bed. "What you mean Otis said?" Asked Cara. Before Vera could answer her, Cotton came through the door carrying Dawn in his arms. Otis and doctor Fox followed.

"Cara I'll have a bed put in here for you to sleep in and your meals brought up to you." Otis told her. "Right now, I want you all to leave while I check and make sure she didn't start bleeding again. All except Cara." Doctor Fox said as he shewed them out the door.

Vera went back to Jacks room and finding him awake. She had him sit on the side of the bed while she changed the sheets. The clean sheets felt cool on Jack as he laid back down and it wasn't long before he was asleep again.

Doctor Fox gave Dawn some laudum for her pain. And Cara gave her a bath, while the doctor prepared fresh bandages for her to put on afterwards.

Jack stayed in bed for two weeks before he was able to get out of it without Cotton and Vera's help. Dawn on the other hand seemed to get better but couldn't move her legs. The doctor said the bullet must have cut a nerve and that was why she didn't have any feeling below her waist. When she asked if she would ever walk again all the doc could say was maybe. Every day that Cara gave her a bath, Dawn would have her pinch her leg, thigh, or hip just to see if she could feel it but it was the same every time.

The overseers didn't like taking orders from Otis but Jack knew that Otis was the only one who could keep the plantation running smoothly in his absence. Cotton became his right-hand man and felt like a king over the rest of the slaves. Sometimes Cotton would abuse his power and get back at the slaves and overseers that had abused him when he was a field hand.

Butch Harder was now living in the Carter place and didn't mind getting his instructions from Jack through Otis. Otis was sitting in the office drinking a glass of whiskey when Cotton came in to tell him that Jack was back on his feet. "Well I knew it wouldn't last forever." He said as he looked around the room then back to Cotton. "What's going to happen to me?" Cotton asked Otis in fear of being sent back to the fields.

"I don't know what Master Jack will do to us." Otis told him. "Do you think I should ask him?" Cotton asked. "If I were you I would just wait until he said something to you." Otis cautioned him. "I think your right. He might think I want to go back the way it was if I say something." Cotton said.

Otis gave a little chuckle. "I don't think he will want that so far he has had his property stolen and he's been shot two times in the last month. I don't think Master Jack wants to go through that again." Otis said. "I guess not." Cotton said with a little laugh of his own.

"Cara go tell Jack I would like to talk to him when he finds the time." Dawn said as Cara finished getting her dressed. Dawn had heard Jack was back on his feet but he hadn't come to see her yet. She didn't know if it was because Sam had tried to kill him or if he felt guilty about her being like she was.

Cara went to find Master Jack but found his room empty. As Cara came out of the room she could hear Vera laughing as she came up the stairs. Cara stood waiting until Vera and Jack made it to the top before she approached them "Master Jack, Miss Dawn would like to talk with you when you have the time." Cara said.

"Okay, you go help Vera clean my room and I'll go see her right now." Jack said. Jack tapped lightly on the door before he entered. Jack put a smile on his face before he entered. Yet found it hard to keep it as he looked at Dawn lying in the bed.

"Jack do you hold what pa did against me?" Dawn asked

"No of course not Dawn. I know you had nothing to do with it or he wouldn't have shot you too." Jack replied.

"Then why haven't you come to see me before now?" Dawn asked. Jack seemed to have trouble finding the right answer before he spoke. "If you would like for me to leave. I'm sure I can find someone to take me in." Dawn said before he had time to answer her first question.

Jack sat down on the side of the bed and took Dawn by the hand. "You'll do no such thing like leave your home. You wouldn't be like this if it wasn't for me." Jack said as his hand waved through the air over Dawn.

"Don't be silly Jack. the reason I'm like this is because my pa tried to kill you and Cotton. I don't want you to feel like you have to keep me here for what pa did." Dawn said with tears in her eyes.

"Damn it Dawn, I'm keeping you here because I love you like a sister." Jack said before he could stop himself.

"I don't want you to love me like a brother Jack. I want you to love me like a man loves a woman." Dawn cried.

"I can't." Jack said as he let go of Dawns hand and rose from the bed.

"Why not. Is it because of this?" Dawn said as she slapped her thigh hard.

"No Dawn. It's because you're my half-sister." He told her. The bullet that Sam had shot her with hadn't hit Dawn as hard as Jacks words. "You're crazy. That bullet must have hit you in the head instead of your back." Dawn said in shock. "I know pa had a lot of slave women but he never had a kid with a white woman. Your mother must have lied to you Jack, so you can't be my brother."

"My mother was a slave girl from this plantation by the name of Maple. She was sold to a whore house in New Orleans where I was born. Sam was my father just like he was yours." Jack said.

"Why are you telling me a story like this? Is it because you want someone else instead of me?" Dawn demanded. Jack came back to the side of the bed. "No Dawn it's because it's the truth. You, me Vera, Cara and Cotton are all fathered by the same man." Jack told her.

"Do you remember that morning we all had breakfast together? Sam got all choked up when I said we were just one big happy family." Jack asked.

"You bastard, you low down bastard. You knew all along and you let me make a fool of myself." Dawn started grabbing things off the night stand and throwing them at Jack. Vera and Cara heard the sound of yelling and glass breaking coming from Dawns room.

"Should we go see what's going on?" Cara asked. "I don't know." Vera said as she turned the door knob to open the door. A hair brush hit the wall beside Jacks head as Vera entered the room.

"What's wrong with her Master Jack?" Vera asked. "It's brother Jack not master Jack." Dawn yelled. "My God she done gone out of her mind." Cara said as she entered the room. "Tell them your lie brother. After all their your sisters too." Dawn said as she looked for something else to throw and found the night stand empty.

Dawn threw back the sheet and slung her legs over the side of the bed. "Tell them how your mother and theirs are sisters." Dawn said as she pushed herself to her feet. Dawn took two steps before she began to fall and Jack caught her in his arms.

Cara didn't understand a thing Dawn was saying, but Vera on the other hand heard every word. "Master Jack, Miss Dawn done lost her mind."

Jack had to lay Dawn in the floor after he had caught her. Otis and Cotton came through the door as Jack laid Dawn down. "Master Jack let me put Miss Dawn back into bed." Cotton said as he bent over to pick her up".Damn you Jack. If you don't tell them I will." Dawn cried as Cotton laid her down in bed. "Tell us what Master Jack?" Cotton asked as he turned to Jack.

All eyes were going from Jack to Dawn as they waited for one of them to speak. "All of you go down to the dining room and wait for me. I will join you there. I have a few things to say to Dawn, then I will tell you." Jack told them. "You all heard Master Jack." Otis said as he ushered them through the door. "Dawn I was going to tell them but I kept putting it off. I'm sorry." Jack said as he left.

Jack could hear the group talking amongst themselves as he approached the dining room. They all fell silent as Jack came in the room. Otis was doing his best to keep order but he was as afraid as the rest that Jack was going to sell them all. Otis' heart almost burst out of his chest when he saw the papers Jack was carrying. He had seen them before and knew they were bill of sales for slaves.

"Master Jack are you going to sell us off?" Otis asked with his eyes on the papers Jack had laid on the table.

"I'm going to tell you a story then I will answer all of your questions." Jack told them. "Otis do you remember a slave named Maple that Sam sold thirty years ago?"

"Yes, Master that's the one that I told you that I didn't know where she went to." Otis said as he rubbed his white hair. "I know what happened to her because I'm her son and Sam was my father. I was born in New Orleans but my mother was born here on this plantation. She was also Sam's daughter." Jack told them.

They all started asking questions but Jack stopped them by raising his hand. "The story begins."

Sam Sarrows finished pouring the remainder of the bottle of whiskey into the glass in his left hand. Then through the bottle into the corner with the crash. Damn Mary. That bitch has been a pain in his ass from the day he married her. The first thing she did was forbid him from bringing a bed wench into the house.

Sam could understand that if she gave him the sex that he craved, but she was so afraid of getting pregnant that she refused to have sex with him. Sam showed her he had the slaves build a long house with beds lining both sides and he had twenty slave girls put in it for his personal use. These girls were hand-picked by Sam like a sultan picks a harem.

Mary knew of his harem but acted like she didn't as long as Sam got his sex from them she didn't have to take the chance of having a baby and dyeing in child birth. Mary was a smart business woman. She learned that when they sold a slave, the lighter it was the more money it brought.

Sam thought of going to pay a visit to his harem but when he tried to get up the whiskey he had drank wouldn't let him. Maybe he would have Otis go fetch him one but if the whiskey wouldn't let his two legs work, then his third leg would be as useless.

Well there was always tomorrow. Sam said as he turned up the glass and downed the rest of the whiskey. The room seemed to spin as he lowered the empty glass. Your lucky bitch. If I could get up to you I'd take what's mine. Sam said in a slurred voice. Sam closed his eyes just to make the room stop spinning. If he didn't he was going to be sick.

"Master Sam, Master Sam, wake up." Sam heard Otis' voice then felt his hand as Otis shook Sam's shoulder. Sam opened his eyes to see Otis standing over him. "Oh, good Otis you can help me to bed." Sam said. "Master you been in this chair all night. It's dawn outside." Otis told Sam. "I'll have a bath brought in you done peed yourself." Otis said.

Sam was surprised to find his legs in working order. Other than his pounding head it was as if the night before never happen. Otis rushed off to have the bath water brought in for Master Sam. Sam made his way up the stairs to the room that held the tub. This was the day that all the girl slaves that turned fourteen was to be brought to the house. Where he kept them for deflowering. After he took their virginity he would decide which ones to keep and which to be sold.

I wish I could sell that bitch of a wife of mine. He said as he slowly lowered himself into the tub of hot water. "Otis how many new girls are supposed to be brought to the house today?" Sam asked Otis. who was laying out his clean clothes. "Five I think Master Sam. Just five."

"One of them is by that Meg that you bought in New Orleans a while back." Otis said. "What's her name?" Sam asked. "Maple, I think, Master. You'll know her. She's as white as cotton and looks just like you." Otis said with a little laugh. "You mean that she is my sucker from Meg? Sam asked.

"Yes, master she sure is yours alright." Otis said. "I might just sell her the way she is. She will bring a lot more if she has not been touched." Otis grunted his agreement. "Has my wife said anything that gives you the idea she knows what's going on." Sam asked Otis. "No Master. Miss Mary never tells me anything because she knows I'll be telling you. She do a lot of talking to Minnie the cook. If she knows you can bet Minnie told her." Otis said. "Ya I'd get rid of Minnie if she didn't know how to cook so good." Sam said to Otis as Otis dried him off.

"How many suckers you got now Master?" Otis asked. "Well let's see. I got two by Meg and one by that girl with green eyes. What's her name Sassy? And two by them wenches I sold last year."

"You sure gave Sassy the right name. That girl would argue with a stump." Otis told Sam as he put down the towel to let Sam get dressed.

Mary was on her way to the dining room when Otis started down the stairs so she waited for Otis to reach the bottom. "Where is that husband of mine?" She asked when Otis reached her.

"He'll be right down Miss Mary. He's just putting on his boots." Otis told her. "From the looks of that room." Mary said pointing toward the den that Sam had spent the night in. "He got too drunk to make it to bed again, didn't he?" Mary asked. Otis answered with a nod of his head. Both Mary and Otis looked to the top of the stairs when they heard the sound of Sam start down them.

Without a word Mary walked away before Sam reached the bottom of the stairs. The two sat in silence for a long time before Mary broke the silence by asking Sam if the food tasted alright. "It tastes the same as it did yesterday." Sam said then fell silent again.

Mary brushed back her blond hair with one hand then brought her coffee cup to her lips with the other. "You know we got to be on the lookout for poison being put in our food." Mary said as she set her cup down.

"Why would Minnie want to do anything like that?" Sam asked with a laugh.

"All I'm saying is we got to keep an eye on them darkies." Mary said. Sam knew that Mary was just trying at conversation. At least she wasn't giving him hell about last night.

"If you like I'll bring a girl in here to eat first and if she lives we can eat in safety." Sam said. He could tell by the look on Mary's face that she wasn't the least bit amused by his attempt at hummer.

"We can start with girls from your little whore house." Mary said as she rose from the table throwing her napkin on the table. Stopping at the doorway she turned and added "I put the poison in myself."

"I sure wish I had listened to my pa about marrying my own cousin." Sam said after Mary left. Just as Sam rose to leave Otis came in and Carter was right behind him. "Sam, we have a problem with that slave Meg. She said that she wasn't going to let her girl Maple come to the house with the others." Carter told Sam. "I could put Maple in chains and give Meg a lashing, but I thought I should talk to you first."

"I'll go to talk to Meg. You just round up the rest of the girls." Sam told him.

"Well ok, but I think if we gave Meg a lashing in front of the others. It will keep them in line." Said Carter.

"Carter, I think you enjoy using the whip too much for a man just doing his job." Sam said.

"Well Sam, there's one thing I found out about my job. If you cut the hide off one nigger in front of a hundred of them, the hundred will do what you tell them without any backtalk." Carter said with a smile.

"Carter, I've raised niggers all my life and there's one thing I've learned. Fear can work both ways. Sam said.

"There your niggers." Carter said as the smile left his face and he turned to leave.

"One of these days that bastard is going to make more trouble than he's worth." Sam said in a low voice even though he was the only one in the room.

Mary meet Sam in the hallway as he came out. "What did that

low-down bastard want?" She asked starring at the door that Carter had just went out. Sam studied Mary to determine what she had heard and decided she knew nothing.

"Oh, he was having some trouble with one of the slaves and wanted to use the whip on him but I told him no." Sam said.

"He hasn't got as much sense as the slaves he's supposed to be watching. Don't he know that every time he uses that whip it costs money?" Mary asked. "You should get rid of him." Mary said as she looked at the door again.

I'd like to get rid of both of you Sam thought as he looked at the back of Mary's head. "One of these days I will." Sam said out loud as he walked off.

"What we going to do when Master Carter comes back?" Maple asked. Meg sat starring out the door of her cabin knowing there was nothing she could do but get in more trouble than she was already in. Meg was supposed to be at the big house cleaning instead of in her cabin waiting for Carter to come take her away in chains and take her daughter Maple to the whorehouse.

"Master Sam won't let Carter put his own girl in that place. Maple you go to Easter's cabin and don't come back until I come for you." Meg told her.

"There's nobody at Easter's cabin. She's at work at the big house by now." Maple told Meg.

"I know that." Meg snapped at Maple.

Maple knew better then to argue with Meg when she was in such a mood. As far as Maple was concerned she would just as soon as go with the other girls and become a woman and get it over with. She didn't understand why her mom was acting like they were being sent to a slaughter house. Maple had talked to some of the older girls and they seemed to like what was done to them at that place.

"Meg, what in hell are you trying to do?" Sam asked as he burst through the door of Meg's cabin.

"Master Sam you not going to put your own child in that horrible place, is you?" Meg cried as she backed up against the wall as far as she could go.

"Meg you are one stupid nigger. Of course, I am. This is a breeding plantation. That's what we do here. Maple may be my daughter but more than that she is my property and I say where she will go and where she will stay." Sam roared.

"Please Master just wait one more summer?" Meg pleaded. "Where is she Meg? Tell me where she is or I'll put both of you on the block next week." Sam said.

Meg had been worried about Maple losing her virginity. She never thought about her being put up for sale. "How long do you think you can keep her hidden?" Sam asked. "Carter wanted to take the whip to you but I told him no. But if you don't tell me, that's just what I'm going to do. Do you hear me?" Sam shouted.

"She's at Easters cabin Master Sam." Meg said pointing to the cabin next door. Meg fell to the floor crying. Sam could hear her crying as he headed for the cabin next door.

Maple was sitting on the bed when Sam came through the door of the cabin. Sam was expecting to find a scared and crying little girl and was surprised when Maple greeted him with a smile. "Morning Master Sam." Maple said sitting on the bed with her hands interlocked and laying in her lap.

smile came to Sam's face. He was expecting to find a light brown girl but Maple was almost as white as he was. If it wasn't for her curly black hair she could pass for a white girl. She looked just like Meg did when he had taken her for the first time except Maple is a shade whiter.

"Girl stand up and take off that sackcloth dress. Sam told her. Maple stood up and quickly pulled off her dress as she had been told. Her small breast were as firm as a marble statue and her butt was round as a melon. Sam could feel how just looking at her caused his blood to boil. He thought of taking her right then but decided to take her to the house and have one of the other girls give her a bath.

"Put your dress back on Maple. I'm going to take you to a place where you can get a bath and a pretty new dress." Sam told her.

"Master Sam, does my new dress have yellow flowers on it? Maple asked in a girlish voice.

"We'll see if I can find you a dress with flowers." Sam said with a laugh.

Meg wanted to scream and run to Master Sam and beg him one more time to let Maple wait one more year. She held herself back by remembering what Sam told her about selling her and Maple too. Just look at Maple, she thinks she is on her way to a party. Maple's joy caused Megs tears to run even harder.

Meg thought back to when she had turned fourteen and how Master Sam came and got her like that. She too thought she was going to a party. How the eyes of the other girls looked at her like she was a white girl. The older girls laughed and the younger girls cried. She could still hear the screams of the girls that went before her. I hope Master Sam shows Maple mercy and makes her go first.

Sam took Maple to the back-kitchen door and told her to wait while he went to find Easter. "Minnie, where's Easter?" Sam asked as he came up behind her.

"Master Sam you done scared the life out of old Minnie." She said after jumping a foot.

"Ya, ya, I know. Now where's Easter?" Sam asked again.

"I'd say she is in Miss Mary's room cleaning." Minnie said.

"You see Meg didn't show up this morning." Sam said.

"I swear that gals been a sack of nerves for the last week. Must be her time." Minnie went on talking without answering Sam.

"Damn it Minnie." Sam said as he put his hand over her mouth to shut her up.

"Go up to Miss Mary's room and tell Easter she is needed in the kitchen." Sam told her.

"But Master Sam, I don't need Easter down here today." Minnie said. Sam put his hand back over Minnie's mouth. "I'm the one that wants her but don't tell her that. Do you understand?" Minnie looked at Sam and shook her head yes. Sam could only imagine what Minnie was mumbling as she left the kitchen and headed for the stairs.

Easter met Minnie at the top of the stairs carrying two buckets of water. "Easter, Master Sam he say he a needing you down in the kitchen." Minnie told her after catching her breath.

"What does Master Sam want? Miss Mary done told me to pack this here bath water out." Easter said as she handed one of the buckets to Minnie.

Sam stood with Maple as Minnie and Easter came into the kitchen. "Minnie go back to work." Sam said as he took the bucket of water from her.

Minnie could tell that Master Sam didn't want her to hear what he was going to say to Easter. That made her all the more determined to hear it so she went to the sink and started doing dishes. The sink was closer to them then the stove. Unless they spoke louder she wasn't going to hear them.

Sam saw what Minnie was doing so he ushered the two girls outside. Sam could swear he heard Minnie say "Shit" as he went out the door.

Easter was two years younger than her sister Meg who was twenty-eight. Even at twenty-six, Easter could excite Sam the way her body stayed looking even after having two kids. "What happened to your mammy?" Easter asked Maple like they were standing at the cabins.

Sam interrupted before Maple could answer. "I want you to take Maple upstairs and give her a bath. Then see if you can find her a clean dress." He told Easter.

"Yellow flowers." Maple said.

"What girl." Easter asked.

"The dress, I want yellow flowers on it." Maple said with a smile.

It occurred to Easter what was going on when he told her not to let Miss Mary see her do it. Easter started to say something but Sam pointed his finger at her to stop her.

"I've done gone through this with Meg and I don't plan to go through it with you, do you hear." Sam said loud enough that Minnie could have heard him anywhere in the kitchen.

"Yes, Master Sam." Was all Easter said before she and maple went back into the house.

Easter managed to get Maple up to the room that held the tub with the left-over bath water. Maple had just entered the room when Mary came out into the hall.

"Ain't you got that tub empty yet?" Mary asked as Easter started to enter the room.

"I'm just about to get finished Miss Mary." Easter said as she ducked into the room.

"You going to get me whipped or sold." Easter said as she closed the door.

"Oh, aunt Easter I would never do that to you." Maple said with a smile. The look Maple gave Easter told her that the girl truly loved her aunt.

"I know you wouldn't do it on purpose, but if Miss Mary nds you up here. She would have Master Carter whip the both of us right before we were put on the block."

"Easter is Master Sam my pa?" Maple asked.

"I'm afraid so child. He is all of us' pa." Easter told Maple to take off that rag she was wearing and get into the tub. Maple had taken a bath in the pond but she had never even seen a for real bathtub before.

Maple quickly jerked off the old sack cloth dress and climbed into the tub of water. Easter knelled beside the tub and with her left hand she rubbed away the tear that rushed down her cheek. With her right hand she picked up the wash cloth and began washing Maple. Easter sucked in a deep breath. "Child do you know what is going to happen to you?" Easter asked in a low voice.

"Sure, aunt Easter I'm going to get a dress with yellow flowers on it." Maple laughed.

Easter fought back her tears the best she could but a few slipped by. "Yes, that too. But in a little while Master Sam is going to take you to a room with a big bed in it. Then he will have you take off your pretty new dress."

"Well I won't do that." Maple told Easter "I'm going to keep on my new dress with yellow flowers."

When Easter couldn't hold back the tears no longer, they burst forth with a vengeance. Easter rose to her feet." I'm tired of treating you like a child Maple. In just a little while you're going to be a woman and I'm going to talk to you like one."

"Easter what did I do to make you so mad at me?" Maple asked as she stood and turned to face Easter.

"I'm not mad at you Maple. I'm just trying to make what's going to happen to you easy." Easters red eyes surveyed Maples long lean body and remembered the day her and Maples mom went through the same thing. "Guess there is no way to prepare you." Easter said and handed Maple a towel. Maple took the towel and studied Easter as she did.

From the look on Easter and her mother's face, maybe what the older girls had told her was not true. She knew a little bit about the difference between a man and a woman. Hadn't she sneaked to the fields and watched all them sweating men at work there. She had to admit the sight of their muscles shinning in the sun light caused a yearning that she didn't understand. "Aunt Easter, I know that a woman only goes through this one time in her life and no matter if its good or bad she only has it for one time." Maple told her aunt like a woman.

"You stay here while I go find you a dress with flowers on it." Easter said. Maple knew that she was just putting on a show for Easter because her insides was turning like a butter churn. Maple was so nerves that she was shacking as she looked at her hands.

Easter was gone only a few minutes but to Maple it felt like hours. "Maple this is the only dress I could find with flowers on it." Easter said as she handed her a white dress with pink roses.

"Oh, this is prettier than the one I wanted aunt Easter." Maple said as she took the dress from Easter and quickly put it on. Maple stood in front of the full-length mirror looking at herself in the dress. the white dress brought out Maples black hair and eyes. She was pretty Easter had to admit.

"Maple you have got to get out of this house before anyone sees you." Easter said as she grabbed her by the arm. Easter lead the way and Maple followed close behind her.

"Who's that?" Minnie asked as the two ran through the kitchen. Maple started to stop and tell her but Easter pulled her on out the door. Once Maple and Easter had made it out the house Easter stopped.

"Maple you go to that long house with all the widows and you will find the other girls." Easter told her.

"Aunt Easter ain't you coming with me?" Maple asked. Easter put her arms around Maple and gave the girl a hug. "No child I'm not. This is something you will have to do on your own." Easter said as she pushed Maple off of her turned and hurried back into the house.

As Maple started walking to the building she had been told to go to. She noticed how all the men looked at her then at the ground. At first, she thought they were playing a game with her, but when Samson the blacksmith who knew her did it. She got mad enough to walk over and ask why.

Samson looked up when he heard Maples voice. "My lord Maple I thought you was a white woman." He told her.

"Well I'm going to be a woman soon. I'm going to the long house like my mother and Easter did a long time ago. Maple saw a blank look replace the smile on Samsons face.

One of the first things a male slave must learn is, you never look at a white woman. If you did it could cost you your life. That was why and the other slaves were looking at the ground when Maple came by. She looked just like a young white girl in her new dress.

Samson knew what house Maple was headed for. He knew all about when a girl turned fourteen she was taken to that house to be bread. Samson had two girls of his own go through it a few years back. "Just remember Maple, the people that love you today will still love you tomorrow." Samson told her before Maple left.

As the long house came into view, so did Joe Carter with a long black bull whip in his hand. While his left hand held the whip, his right hand had a girl by the hair dragging her toward the house screaming and crying. Maple knew Carter on sight. She remembered how he tried to feel her breast when she didn't have any. She had told him that she was going to tell Master Sam so he picked a stick up off the ground and chased her away.

"Get your ass in there." Joe said as he pushed the struggling girl through the door. Joe didn't see the pretty white girl walking toward him until she was almost to the door. "Woo, woo, there young lady.

You can't go in there." Joe said as he tried to block her way.

Maple backed up a few feet and looked at the building to make sure she was at the right place.

"Miss you shouldn't be out here without a man with you. You should have had Otis come with you. Has any of these black bastards done anything to you?" Joe asked Maple.

"Well I had my aunt walk with me but she had to go back to work." Maple said. Joe's eyes widened and his mouth Few open when he realized who he was talking to.

"You Meg's girl? You is a slave? I'll be damned. You sure don't look like a slave in that dress." Joe said with a roaring laugh. "I'll bet old Sam will forget about them other girls when you go in there. After he's had his fill of you. I'll be seeing you pretty." Joe said as he stepped out of Maples way.

Maple hadn't known fear until she went through that door that day. Up until then, the plantation had been her safe place. Her home. It wasn't until a few weeks ago that Meg had set her down and told her that the place she had always called home was a breeding plantation. A place where they grew people instead of cotton.

Meg explained that a man and woman was put into the same bed and they try to make a baby. Meg had went on to say that I was becoming the age that the Master shows you what you are living on his plantation. Maple hung her head and drawled a line in the dirt with her toe.

"Mama I don't know how to have a baby. Will the master putts me on the block?"

Meg placed her hand on the back of Maples head and stroked her long black hair. "It won't make Master Sam mad because you don't know how to make a baby. He will take pleasure in showing you." Meg said looking toward the big house even though you couldn't see it from the cabin.

The black girl that Joe had by the hair sat in one corner with another girl Maple had never seen before crying. There was another girl by the name of Rosezita but everybody called her Rose. She had been captured in Mexico and sold to Master Sam. Rose wasn't crying but she looked to Maple like she couldn't stand still.

Maple walked closer to Rose and could see that Rose had bit her nails to the quick. "Rose?" Maple said as she touched her on the shoulder.

"Master Sam just took a friend of mine back there." Rose said pointing to a room at the back of the building.

Master Sam's voice broke the silence. "Now girl I don't have all day. Take off them clothes and lay down on that bed." She heard him say.

The sound of Sam's voice caused the two girls in the corner to start crying so loud that Maple couldn't hear what Master Sam was saying. Shush Maple said to the girls in the corner and they seemed more afraid of Maple then what they were crying about. Maple never thought no more about it. until much later. But the two crying slaves thought she was a white lady and everyone knew that Rose was a Mexican.

The room fell silent for a few minutes then a hair-raising scream filled the room. Maple and rose through themselves into each other's arms. Maple couldn't hold back her tears no longer, when scream after scream came from that room. Maple knew that Master Sam wasn't the one doing them.

She was really certain when Sam shouted for the girl to stop all that damn screaming. The girl stopped screaming but she couldn't hide her crying. It had been Maples plan to go in there and get it over with until now. Maple looked at the two girls in the corner and guessed that their silence was what had caught her attention. They looked like they had died sitting up. The only way you could tell they wasn't dead was when you saw them take a breath. Then the sound of Master Sam's voice telling the girl to get dressed and get out.

The ground was packed hard where Meg had paced back and forth in front of the cabin. She was preparing to deal with a girl that had been rapped. "Meg it's better to have a daughter that's been rapped then to have her put on the block." She told herself as she paced. Meg heard Joe Carter and his whip before she saw him. She heard the whip snap then Carter order someone to get back inside. The hairs on the back of Megs neck stood up when a big grin came to Carters face when he saw her.

"Now Meg, you know that your little girl is just starting what she was put here for." Joe said as he walked up to Meg.

"I know Master Carter but she is so young." Meg said as Carter came to a stop. "Can I help you with something Master Carter?" Meg asked.

"You sure can." Joe said as he stroked her hair. Meg stepped away from Joe.

"Now Master Carter, Master Sam won't let me do nothing like that." She said.

"Sam's got himself breaking in the new girls. They will keep him at it for a while. What you say we go into your cabin and talk about it." Joe said as he shook the whip at Meg.

All thought of what was happening to Maple left Meg. She knew exactly what Master Carter had on his mind and she was powerless to stop him. "You know as well as I do that Sam hasn't been with you for over a year." Carter said as he directed Meg into the cabin. "Shuck that dress Meg." Carter said as he closed the door.

Megs hands trembled as she tried to undo the string that held her sack cloth dress to stay on. "Now Meg don't you act like you is your daughters age. This ain't your first time." Carter said.

It was true that Master Sam was the only man she had ever had but how many times had Sam taken her over the last fourteen years. The dirty sack cloth dress fell to the floor at Megs feet.

Joe Carters toothless grin returned as his eyes locked on Meg, like a rabbit under the paws of a hungry wolf. "You still got a shape for a thirty-year-old. No one would think you done had four youngins." Joe said as he approached Meg.

"Master Sam will get powerful mad when he finds out you be pestering his girl." Meg told Joe as he drew nearer.

"Sam's not going to say a thing about it because if the people knew he was doing it too they would lynch him." That was the first time that Meg ever realized that the white people thought what Sam was doing was wrong too.

Meg stood five foot five, and weighed one hundred and twenty-eight pounds and Joe was about the same height but outweighed 125 lbs. or more. Meg thought about putting up a fight but decided that the only one who would get hurt was her.

"Get on that bed now Meg." Joe said as he took off his pants. Megs eyes were filled with tears as she did as she was told. "By the time I'm finished Meg you will come looking for me the next time." Joe laughed as he climbed on top of Meg.

As the crying girl came out of the room, the other girls looked at each other to determine who was next. Maple saw that all three girls were looking at her. Maple took the back of her hand and wiped the tears away from her eyes, took a deep breath then started walking to the back room.

Sam's eyes caught Maple walking towards him. "Woo there girl. What's your hurry?" Sam asked as he reached for the jug of moonshine setting on the floor by the door.

Maple stopped dead in her tracks hoping this old man was through for the day. Sam rested the jug on his forearm while he took about three swallows then took down the jug. "I know you you're that girl I left with Easter this morning ain't you?" Sam asked.

"Yes, Master I'm Maple and Easter is my aunt and Meg is my mother." Maple said.

"I can say one thing for Meg, she sure makes a pretty sucker." Sam said as he set the jug back on the floor. Maple closed her eyes and caught a big breath then started walking toward the room. "No not you. You go back to Megs and wait there for me." Sam said pointing his finger at Maple.

Maple was both relieved and disappointed at the at the same time. She was relieved she didn't have to go through with it in front of the other girls. Disappointed that she couldn't just get it over and done with it.

"Ha you standing behind her, you're that Indians from Mexico ain't you?" Sam asked Rose who was standing in the shadows behind Maple.

"Yes Master Sam." Rose said in a broken voice as she stepped into the light.

"Your next." Sam said pointing toward the room. "Tell Carter to get in here as you go out." Sam told Maple to her back as she headed out the door.

Roses black eyes locked onto Sam's blue ones as she walked past him. Sam couldn't understand it but when he looked into her eyes the hair on the back of his neck stood up.

"There's one thing about you Indians, you don't keep your looks for long. So, I'm going to get my money's worth quick." Sam said as he reached out and squeezed Roses young breast. Sam could see the flames of hell in her eyes.

Easter stood outside Miss Mary's door trying to decide on whether to knock on the door or not. Meg must be going out of her mind by now and Easter wanted to go to her. Her older sister Meg had a bad experience when Master Sam took her virginity. Before Easter could stop it, her hand was knocking on Miss Mary's door.

"Come in." The voice said from the other side. Mary looked up from her reading as Easter came in to her room. "What is it Easter?" Mary asked in a harsh voice.

"Miss Mary, I would like to go see my sister if you will let me?" Easter asked.

"What's the reason she didn't come to work this morning? Is she sick?" Mary asked.

"Oh yes mam. She powerful sick this morning. She thinks she might be knocked." Easter told her.

From the look on Mary's face, Easter thought just maybe, should have used a different lie.

"You finish your work then you can go." Mary said as she went back to reading.

"Thank you, Miss Mary. I'll do that, I sure will." Easter said as she left.

Maple walked slow so her feet wouldn't kick up much dust on her pretty white dress with pink roses. Just wait until her mom saw it. She would want to take it and put it away. Maple looked at the dress then at what the rest of the slaves wore around her. The men wore burlap britches and the women wore dresses made of feed sack cloth.

As Maple saw their cabin come into view, she could see that the door was closed. Her mom must have gone to work after all. Maple froze in her tracks as she entered the cabin. Joe Carter had Megs hands pined by the wrist with one hand and slapping her with the other hand.

"You bitch! You had better move like you got some life in you or I'm going to get that bull whip! I bet you do some moving then." Joe said pointing toward the whip lying on the floor. Carter hadn't noticed Maple until he heard her gasp. "Well now." He said as he tried to get off the bed.

"Maple get out of here!" Meg screamed as she wrapped her legs around Joe trying to hold him until Maple could get away.

"Let go Bitch!" Joe said as his big fist slammed into Megs right eye. Meg went limp as a wet rag and fell back into bed. Something told Maple to get as far away as she could but her legs wouldn't move. In a flash Joe was standing in front of her with his hand on her shoulder.

"No Master Carter I'll move for you." Meg pleaded as she got off the bed. Her right eye had done swollen shut and a stream of red blood came from her mouth. Joe Carter laughed at how Meg looked like a whipped dog trying to protect a pup.

"You just sit your ass in that corner and me and this pretty little thing is going to show you how it's done." Joe roared.

"Run Maple!" Meg was able to say before Joes fist found its mark again.

Maple turned to run but Joes hand grabbed her shoulder tight and as she turned Joes finger pulled hard on her white dress and the material gave way under his strength and ripped.

The fear she felt this morning was nothing to what she felt now. This morning she was in fear of losing her virginity now she was in fear for her life. The dress ripped from Maple's shoulder to her waist and the force of Joe's hand through Maple from where she was standing to the bed five foot away. Maple was like a fat stone being skipped across water. She bounced up against the wall.

Joe walked to the bed and got a grip on the ripped dress and pulled on the torn cloth and ripping the dress the rest of the way off. Maple was struggling to catch her breath after hitting the wall. That she didn't realize that she was laying there completely nude.

"Oh my God! You done killed my baby!" Meg cried trying to reach Maple from the corner.

"She's not dead." Joe said as he drew back his hand telling Meg that she had better stay in the corner. The first thing Maple saw after she was able to catch her breath was Joe Carter looming above her.

"Get that dress off and lay on the bed." Sam said as he followed her into the room "How come your not crying your eyes out like the others?" Sam asked as he neared the bed.

"Because in my village we have a saying, do not waste your tears over something you cannot change."

"Smart girl." Sam said as he reached for Rose.

"That includes death." Rose said as she brought her knee up between his legs. Sam was bent over double when he hit the floor with a thump.

"You little bitch! You as good as dead!" Sam was finally able to say after catching his breath.

"Don't let her get away Carter!" Sam yelled as Rose ran from the room. Sam was only able to get to his knees before vomit poured from his mouth like a fountain.

Rose was surprised to see there was no Joe Carter to be seen anywhere as she came out.

"Get her Joe! Don't let her get away!" Sam said as he pulled himself to his feet.

Fear didn't hit Rose until she reached the outside. Where are you going? She asked as she ran as fast as she could.

Maple could feel Joe's fingers grip behind each knee and pulled her legs apart. Maple tried her best to jerk her legs free but Joes grip was just too strong.

"Oh, baby don't fight him. That's what he wants." Meg cried from the corner. Maple didn't know she could make such a sound as what came out of her mouth as Joe penetrated her. Her first thought was that she had been stabbed with a knife down there. She tried to put as much distance between her and him. Joe Carter just laughed and pulled her even further onto him.

Maple knew the tears she was crying was because her body was starting to respond to Joe's brutality. By the time Joe had finished his attack Maples hips was rising to meet the thrust she knew was coming. Maples whole body shook as she experienced a feeling that was totally new to her. With eyes closed and head raised Joe ground his release. His eyes few open at the sound of the door slamming open against the wall.

Sam had sent Apalo the blacksmith to find Joe Carter. He had been walking with Easter when he heard the scream. Apalo rushed past Easter and came face to face with Master Carter. "And what do you think your going to do boy?" Joe asked as he pulled up his pants. Joe could see the anger in Apalo's eyes but knew that no slave would raise a hand to a white man for fear of death.

Apalo swallowed hard then told Joe that Master Sam was needing him fast. "Fat Indian girl done run off into the swamp."

"Dumb little bitch doesn't know she'll be gator bait in the swamp. She'll be dead before night fall." Joe said.

Maple was sorting out what had just happened to her when she heard Roses name and that got her attention. Maple hadn't noticed both Meg and Easter trying to comfort her. "Why oh why does Master Sam keep that animal stay around here? Easter asked as she wrapped the torn dress around Maple's shoulders.

"He's going to track Rose like a deer and kill her dead ain't he?" Maple asked.

Sam was laying in the bed in pain as Joe entered the room. The two slave girls huddled in the corner afraid to make a sound caught Joe's eyes as he entered the room.

"Where were you Carter? You was supposed to be outside just in case something like this happened." Sam asked.

"I had to go pee. I was on my way back when Apalo found me." Joe replied. Sam shook his head because he didn't believe a word of what Carter was saying. Right now, he had more important things to attend to. "Well before you got to go pee again, do you think you can get a few overseers and some slaves to go after that little bitch and bring her back here."

"Sure Sam. I'll have her back before dark." Joe said. Sam had forgot about the two girls in the corner until Joe walked out.

"What the hell you two still doing here? Get out!" Sam said pointing toward the open door. The two girls ran for the open door as fast as they could run not even looking back. Just the thought of sex made Sam hurt.

After Otis got Sam to the upstairs bedroom without Mary seeing them, Sam thought he was safe from an endless line of questions. "Otis go down stairs and bring me that jug of whiskey setting on that shelf. Be sure you get the right one." Sam said as Otis went out the door.

"I'll have that little bitch tied down and make every breading buck I got have a go at her. Then I'm going to sell her to the highest bidder." Sam gently cupped his swollen stratum as he talked to himself.

Sam had just noticed that Otis had left the door open when Mary's face appeared in it. "What you doing up here in bed this time of day?" Mary asked as her eyes scanned the room for a slave girl.

Sam quickly jerked his hand away from himself before he answered. "I just got to much sun, so I came in to cool off." Sam said.

"Would you like a glass of lemon aid?" Mary asked. "No, I'm going to drink some water." Sam said as he looked at the water pitcher.

"What has happened to all the help this morning? Meg didn't show up. Then Easter wanted to get off early to go see about Meg, and I have no idea where Otis is." Mary was saying as she walked to get Sam a glass of water.

Just then Otis came through the door carrying a jug of shine. Sam smiled when he realized why he thought so much of Otis. "Master Sam is this the right jug you want me to take to Master Carter?" Otis asked.

"Yes, that's the right one." Sam said with a grin. He knew that Otis would take the jug away until Mary had left, then bring it back to him.

Otis knew where the power was around the plantation. Miss Mary could make it hard on him but Master Sam could have him put back into the fields or whipped to death and that brought Otis loyalty. Otis had been Master Sam's slave since he had been twelve, now he's thirty. Otis saw a glass of whiskey as he set the jug back on the shelf.

"I bet I'm the only slave living on a breeding plantation who don't get sex." Otis said just before emptying the glass. The girls that worked in the house was Master Sam's daughters and he couldn't tell Easter how pretty he thought she was.

"Do you think we should tell Master Sam." Easter asked as she bathed Megs eye.

"No no. It would do no good to tell Master Sam. Because Master Carter said he knew something about Master Sam so he wouldn't do anything." Meg said.

"I guess your right. Besides everyone will know about it when they see you at work tomorrow." Replied Easter.

"I can't go around Miss Mary and Master Sam like this." Meg said pointing at her face.

"Meg you will have to go to work tomorrow or Miss Mary will come after you herself sick or not." Easter told Meg. Meg knew Easter was right. If she missed another days work Miss Mary would come and get her. The only thing Meg could do was tell Mary what happened and maybe she would get rid of him.

Maple sat and stared out the door thinking of how her and Rose had been friends from the time Rose had arrived. Maple hoped this was all a bad dream and she would wake up. She remembered how she and Rose would sneak down to where the field hands washed and spy on them. Another tear came to Maples eye as she remembered how brutal Master Carter could get.

Who ever said Indians don't cry didn't know what they were talking about. Rose thought as she sat on a mound of dry dirt that stuck up out of the green water. Rose had watched a little deer that had come to get a drink get eaten by a fifteen-foot crock.

What she had done this morning was so stupid that Rose couldn't believe she had done it. The only thing she had accomplished was to either get eaten by the crock or get taken back and whipped to death.

The sound of a big fish flopping took Roses attention to where she had just came through the swamp. The green water had a dark black cloud of bottom mud leading straight to her. Roses heart pounded in her chest as she looked at the mud. It was like drawing a line straight to her that a blind man could follow. How could she go on without leaving a trail for them to follow? Her eyes searched for a fallen tree that went from one island to another one. A smile came to Roses face as her eyes rested on one.

The crock was finishing off what was left of the little deer so Rose used the time to move from the little island to a bigger one. The fallen tree was so old that all the bark was gone off it and Roses feet had a hard time keeping traction on it and was slipping constantly.

"Damn." Rose said after she reached the other island and looked back the way she had came. The tree she had used was wet from her dress. She could see where the dress had got against was wet making the dark wood stand out from the other trees. Rose reached down and grabbed the hem of her dress and pulled it up over her head. After Rose rolled the dress in to a ball making it easier to carry, she broke off some swamp grass and rubbed out her tracks. The afternoon sun made the swamp like a sweat bath from the humidity.

Rose thought of something she hadn't planned on and that was where she could get drinking water and food. It was almost dark before Rose stopped to rest. As she sat down and leaned with her back against the tree. The sound of baby birds in a nest caught her attention.

"The little bitch just disappeared." Joe Carter was telling Sam as he stood by Sam's bed.

"Now Carter, I've lived here by this swamp my whole life and no matter what animal goes through that swamp leaves a trail." Sam said.

"Sam I'm telling you. We followed her straight to a island no bigger than this room and she left no trail showing how she left."

Sam's blue eyes fell on Joe. "I can't afford to have so many men out chasing one young girl. So I'll tell you what you are going to do Carter. You are going to take two bucks and go find that girl and if you don't find her don't come back. Do you hear?"

"Now you hear me Sam. I'll go try to find that girl but I'll come back here anytime I get ready or would you prefer for me to go to tell Miss Mary that you tried to higher me to kill her?" Joe said as his blue eyes locked on Sam's.

"Now Joe there's no need for you to bring that up. You know that I'm just hurting is all." Sam knew that Joe had him over a stump.

Maple stood in the doorway looking out over the swamp as the sun set."Rose I wish you had told me what you were going to do, I'd went with you."

Easter had taken Meg to her cabin so Maple could have some time alone and still be close enough if she needed them. Maple thought that once Master Sam found out what Master Carter did to her, he would have him whipped. That was foolish of her to even think that it didn't matter which white master robbed her of her virginity. She would be put in a long house with a lot of other girls and bread like a horse or cow. The only way out of that would be to start working in the big house where it was safe. At least her mom had been safe until today. Maple had heard all the stories her mom had told about Miss Mary but she had never been treated like this. I want to get somewhere I'll never have to have sex again. The only way she saw to working in the house was to go to Miss Mary.

It had been two months since that awful day that Maple had been attacked and Rose ran off. Maple was all set to go tell Miss Mary but her mom and aunt Easter told her to keep her mouth shut or she would be put on the block just to shut her up. "Honey child, these is white folks we're talking about." Meg told Maple. "If you want to stay on this plantation you don't say a word to a white person to another white person. the only one that gets hurt is you."

What her mother said made sense to Maple. It was true she wanted to get back at Master Carter, but she had heard enough stories from the other slaves that she knew there were places a lot worse than where she was. Maple placed a hand on her stomach and looked down. It was coming upon two months since she had had her time of month. When she missed the first month she just put it off to what she had gone through. It was two days from the time she should have started but hadn't.

A smile came to Maples face as she thought that she might have a little girl growing inside her right now. The smile soon left her face when she thought of what her little girl would have to go through. Aunt Easter had talked to Miss Mary and got her a job of working in the kitchen with the cook. The funny part of her job was when the cook got the meal finished, Maple was to sample everything and tell Miss Mary what it tastes like.

Maples hand went back to her swollen belly, as she patted it said, it's because of all the food she had been eating. Maple had no sooner gone through the kitchen door when Minnie told her to get a bucket of hot water and start plucking the chickens. Maple knew that Minnie didn't like her but she didn't know why. Every time Maple tried to talk to her she would send her to do another little job. AS Maple dipped the hot water from the kettle, she was surprised to turn and see Master Sams blue eyes looking at her.

"Well there you are." Sam said as he approached her. "Miss Mary told me you were working in the kitchen now. I didn't believe her until I saw you here. Knowing how she feels about sucker's that belong to me but here you are." "Yes Master Sam. I been here for two weeks, I think." Maple said with a forced smile.

"Look Maple, you know not to say anything to Miss Mary about what happened between us." Sam told Maple.

"Master Sam nothing happened between us." Maple told Sam.

A grin came to Sam's face. "Girl tell everyone that the sucker you are packing belongs to someone else." Sam said pointing to her belly.

"I'll tell her it belongs to Master Carter, Master Sam."

Sams belly jiggled as he laughed. "You do that, that's exactly what you tell her." Sam said as walked off laughing.

Maple had to set the bucket of water down before she dropped it. Master Sam had just confirmed what she, herself was thinking she was with child. One thing Master Sam was good at was spotting a girl with child. That meant Master Carters baby because she hadn't been touched since the attack.

Maple was staring off into space fighting the feelings she was having. First, she would get excited thinking of having a little girl of her own. Then she would get depressed thinking her baby would be treated like breeding stock. She was so deep in thought that she didn't see Otis walk up to where she was setting.

"Are you alright?" Otis asked. A smile came back to Maples face when she saw Otis. Of all the people in the big house he was the only one that Maple could call friend. "Yes, Otis. I'm fine. I was just thinking about being a mother someday."

"You best put that off as long as you can." Otis told her.

"Once you start having suckers a women's body kinda starts pointing toward the ground." Otis said with a laugh.

The smile left Maples face, "I never thought of that." Maple said.

"What I came here for is Miss Mary told me to bring you to her room." Otis said. Maple couldn't explain the goose bumps that came to her arms. It wasn't time for her to give her report about the food yet.

Maple tapped lightly on Miss Mary's door hoping she would be asleep or gone. "Come in." Came a voice from the other side.

"Miss Mary, Otis told me that you wanted me." Maple told Mary.

"That's right. I have a little errand for you." Mary said as she handed Maple a list of names. "Take this list to Master Carter and tell him it's the list of slaves to be taken to New Orleans." Mary said handing her the list.

Maple fell to her knees. "Oh Miss Mary please don't make me go near Master Carter. Oh please!" Maple begged. Mary could see the girl was frightened out of her whits. I know that Carter has a few bad habits but this child acts like she was being sent to hell to give a message to the devil. "Come here child and sit." Mary said as she patted the chair beside her.

Maple slowly rose to her feet and went to the chair. "Now tell me what Carter did to make you act like you do." Mary said.

Maple placed her hand on her belly. She didn't know if it was because of what she was going to tell Miss Mary or if it was the baby. Maple sat without saying a word for a few minutes thinking of the warning her mother had gave her about talking to white people. As Maple looked at Miss Mary tears filled her eyes.

"Master Carter had came to our cabin and he had been drinking a jug of moon. I had been out walking and when I returned he was having his way with my mother and when I saw them I couldn't move. He grabbed me and tore off my dress, threw me on the bed and had his way with me. Now I'm going to have a baby." Maple said as she looked down at her belly.

"Tell me the truth, had you ever been with a man before?" Mary asked. "No Miss Mary I was a virgin when he did that." Maple replied.

"Damn that low down bastard. He cost us at least a thousand dollars." Mary said as she rose from her chair.

"You go back to the kitchen and I'll take this to Mr. Carter myself." Mary said as she took back the paper. Maple didn't understand why she didn't feel better after telling Miss Mary about what happened but for some reason she felt like her troubles was just beginning. Maple met Easter as she was going to the kitchen and told her what she had done.

"Oh my God child. You shouldn't have done that." Easter scolded. Mary found Joe Carter just getting ready to leave with two slaves in a boat looking for Rose. "Mr. Carter you have cost this plantation a thousand dollars by attacking that Maple. I'm going to have Sam run you off this place."

"What are you talking about?" Joe asked.

"By forcing yourself on that virgin you cost us a thousand dollars." Mary said angrily.

"I never forced myself on no virgin." Joe said in a voice that told he honestly believed it.

"That poor child is with child and she said you are the father."

"That girl was no virgin. She had just come from the breeding house when I took her." said Joe.

"I don't believe you. She has no reason to lie to me about it." Replied Mary.

"Look Miss Mary I haven't got time to tell you what happened right now, but I will when I get back with that girl that ran off."

"I'm telling you, I will get to the bottom of this. If your lying I will fire you. If that girl is lying then I will sell her, is that clear." Mary said as she turned to go.

"You do that Miss Mary. You just do that." Joe said as he climbed into the boat. "Ask Sam about that girl." Joe said as the two slaves rowed away.

Rose had traveled through the swamp for two days without food or water before she met a tall man as black as coal on the third day. She was weak from hunger thinking about trying to make it back to the plantation when the big black man appeared from the brush. Thinking he was sent to bring her back she wanted to get up and run but was just too weak.

"Don't be afraid of me girl. I won't hurt you."

"They will kill me if you take me back." Rose said.

The big black let out a roaring laugh. "I'm not going to take you back to them white devils. I'm here because I run two years ago. You must be needing water and food by now." He said as he took a bag of water from his shoulder and handed it to Rose.

Rose drank from the bag until the man grabbed it back from her. "You should drink just a little or you'll get sick." Rose couldn't understand why this man was being cruel by teasing her. was he just something her tourchered mind had made up or was he real?

"Come with me." He said as he started back the way he had come. Rose just sat until he turned and asked if she wanted something to eat.

Driven by hunger more than fear, Rose got to her feet and began following him. Rose followed him for what seemed like hours to her before they came to a cave set high on a hill. The man stopped at the entrance and reached out his hand to Rose.

"It's dark in here and you might get lost." He said when Rose just stood there. "If I was going to hurt you I would have done it by now." He said. Rose took his hand as he led her into the darkness of the cave.

Rose could smell the smoke from his fire before she saw its light. Whoever this man was he had been living here for a long time she could tell by the blackness the smoke had left on the ceiling of the cave. "My name is Kodar but the whites call me Zeus." He said as he motioned for Rose to sit down. "I was ten years old when my village was attacked by the whites and we were put into chains."

Rose started to say something but Kodar just kept on talking. "My life as a slave has been more painful for me because of my people's reputation as head hunters.

Sam was sitting in his office when Mary came through the door. "Sam there's something I've got to talk to you about." She said as she came around his desk.

"What is it this time?" He asked Mary.

"It's about that Joe Carter. I want you to get rid of him, he has attacked that new girl and got her pregnant."

Sam leaned back in his chair and laughed. "Mary this is a breeding plantation. That's what we do here." Sam told her with a bigger laugh.

"I know Sam but he took a virgin and that cost us a thousand dollars or more." Mary said as she sat down in his lap. could tell that Mary was offering herself if he would do what she wanted. If he played his cards right. Sam could get past that wall Mary had put between them at least for tonight. Sam brought his right hand up and cupped Mary's left breast. "I'll have a talk with Carter when he gets back." Sam said as he squeezed.

"I don't want you to talk to him. I want you to get him off this place!" Mary said as she jumped to her feet.

"Ok, ok, I'll get rid of him." Sam said as he hooked his arms around Mary's hips and placed his head on her stomach.

"Sam." Mary said as she broke his grip and stepped back. "Don't you get enough of that with them slave girls?" Mary asked. She could see flames of anger come onto Sam's blue eyes as he shot out of the chair.

"This has nothing to do with sex Mary, I'm getting up in years and so are you. I want a son to hand this over to someday. I can't get a son without you." Sam told her.

"Sam you have more kids around here that you can't know how many are yours. Between you and that Joe Carter, we have more white slaves then black ones." Mary shot back.

"You know I will not give this to a nigger. No matter how white he is." Sam yelled.

"Just give me a little more time Sam. Just a while longer." Mary said as she turned to go.

"Mary I will have an heir. Even if I have to marry another woman to do it." Sam said as he sat back down.

"Master Sam." Otis said as he tapped on the open door facing.

"Yes, Otis what is it?" Sam askedaster Sam there's a man here from New Orleans to talk to you."

"Okay, show him in and close the door." Sam said staring out the window.

Maple was doing her work in the kitchen when she saw Otis come in with a look of dread. "Maple, Miss Mary wants you to come to her room right away."

"What's this all about." Maple asked.

"I don't know child but she's in a bad mood." Otis said.

Meg was in the hallway as Maple drew near Miss Mary's door. "Mom what's this all about." Maple asked.

"I'm not sure but I was told to come up here with you." Meg replied. When the two entered the room, Mary was sitting in the chair with her back to them. "Miss Mary you wanted to see us?" Meg asked.

"Yes, I do." Mary said as she turned around. "Meg when you came in here a few months ago with that black eye you told me that you accidentally hurt yourself isn't that right."

"Yes, Miss Mary I told you that." Agreed Meg.

"You lied to me, didn't you? You got that eye from Mr. Carter when he attacked you." accused Miss Mary.

"Yes Miss Mary, but I did it so I could just forget about that day." Meg said.

"The fact that you lied to me is what I'm talking about. No matter why you did it doesn't matter." Mary's eyes fell on Maple. "And you girl, you told me the truth but I have decided that both of you will be taken to New Orleans. Master Sam is going to get rid of Mr. Carter and you two will be put on the block."

"Oh, please Miss Mary! Do with me what you want' being the

liceing dog that I am. But don't put Maple on the block. She has done nothing wrong." Meg pleaded as she dropped to her knees.

"Master Sam and I decided to get rid of all of you and put this matter behind us."

"Please Miss Mary just whip us and put us in the fields and you won't have to see us no more. Meg pleaded.

"My mind has been made up. Your tears won't change a thing. I'm telling you now so you can tell your friends good bye and get your things in order." Mary said.

Maple was more frightened by seeing her mom on her knees begging, then by what Miss Mary was saying.

"I will be going to New Orleans with Sam and Mr. Carter and Sam and I will be the only one's coming back." Mary said. Maple started to say that this was all her fault but Mary held up her hand to stop her. "Now go to your cabin and stay until we are ready to go."

Meg got to her feet still crying and lead Maple from the room.

Joe Carter was surprised to see Sam standing at the boat dock as they came to shore. "I see you didn't find her again Carter. I was hoping to take that little bitch to New Orleans with us and put her on the block." Sam said.

"There was no sign of her anywhere. I'll say she got eaten by a crock or sunk in quicksand." Joe said.

"I guess you're right." Sam said as Carter got out of the boat. "The reason I'm here is to tell you that you will be going with us to New Orleans next week. We have also added two more names to the list."

"What two did you add?" Carter asked.

"Meg and Maple." Sam said.

"They should bring a good price from some whore house down there." Joe said with a laugh. "Getting rid of that Maple before she tells Miss Mary that you're the daddy of that sucker, are you?"

"That's none of your concern." Sam told Carter.

At first Maple was so taken by the beauty of New Orleans that she forgot why they had been brought there. Her life on the plantation was the only part of the world she knew. As the wagons they rode in passed by the brick buildings with great white columns and rows of ships setting in the gulf. The water seemed to reach the sky with no end. Meg was just as caught up in so many people that walked the streets as Maple was in the houses.

A young white girl, not much bigger then Maple, pointed her finger and asked her mother "Why is that white girl riding with them niggers?" Her mother slapped her hand and said it's not polite to point.

Maple felt of the chain the connected her leg irons to the other slaves. If it wasn't for this I could just jump out and run away into the city, Maple thought. The sound the wagon wheels made on the cobble stone street suddenly ended as they turned onto a dirt lane leading to the holding pens. Maple could smell the stench of the pens before she saw them. Only the wagons carrying the slaves went to the stock pens. Sam and Mary went on to the hotel. Joe Carter was in charge of getting the slaves put in the cells each made of blacks with a thick wooden door.

The men were put in one cell and women put in a different one. Maple and Meg entered what seemed like a large barn that held a hundred or more slaves that had come off the ships outside. Most of them didn't speak the same language. Some of the slave girls thinking Meg and Maple were white came to beg for their freedom.

Not knowing their language both Meg and Maple could tell what they wanted with their gestures. The only light in the large room came from a little window at the top of the wall. Meg and Maple found a space in a small part of the building and sat down. Maple found out that she was more afraid of the slaves then she was of the masters. All the women from the plantation made their way to one place for they were just as afraid as Meg and Maple. Even the two slaves that didn't get along on the trip there sat together.

Sam took the most expensive room in the hotel had to offer. It was his plan to please Mary into letting him create an heir. He just knew that if he gave into his demands that she would give him a son. She had been tolerable on the trip down, going as far as kissing him before getting into the bed she had fixed for her in the wagon. Sam made sure that the room he rented just had one bed in it, he was no dummy. He told her to stand by the stair case while he got the room. They just had one left he told Mary as they started up the stairs.

"Oh, this is a nice room." Sam told her as he gave the bellhop a penny.

"I guess it will have to do." Mary said as she took off her bonnet that came from France.

"Just look at how shinny that brass chamber pot is." Sam said pointing to the foot of the bed. Mary looked to where Sam was pointing and started laughing. Sam's reflection made him look like a man with a little head, a pot belly, and long legs. Mary couldn't stop herself from laughing.

"What in Sam hell are you laughing at?" He asked.

"At that." Mary said as Sam came up beside her pointing to the reflection. Sam looked up to see that the bed canopy was hiding the mirror that covered the bed from post to post.

"Look here Mary, you can watch what's going on when I make my son." Sam said with a big grin.

"My God Sam. I really don't want to do this, let alone watch it in a mirror." Mary could see the anger flash in Sams eyes.

"Watching it or not woman, you will give me a son." Sams voice told Mary that his mind was set and that she would be had before the night was over. Mary's fist clenched by her side.

"Only if I say so." Mary shot back, as she stood her ground. "Now down to something more important." Mary said as she undid her fist and sat down on the side of the bed. "Have you told Joe Carter that he is not coming back with us?" Mary asked.

"No, I haven't told him yet. I'm going to wait until the slaves are sold before I tell him." Mary had to admit that was the best thing to do.

"Well Sam I guess you're right. It's better to use Carter as long as possible before we fire him. What's in there?" Mary asked pointing to a door on the far wall.

Sam walked over and opened the door. The little room was completely white with a big brass tub with its own water supply. Sam walked in and turned one of the two handles that stuck out of the wall by the tub. "I'll be damn." Sam said as he stuck his hand into the hot water now filling the tub.

"Oh yes!" Mary said as she started taking her dusty clothes off. She had gotten three buttons undid before she saw how Sam was watching her. "You go have a drink or something." She told Sam as she motioned for him to leave.

The sign that hung beside the two swinging doors read, Whiskey Women and Poker. Joe Carter couldn't read a lick but knew what the sign said. He had been here a lot of times and it would give him everything he was looking for. He knew the owner Jake Benson for years now and had sold him slaves of questionable ownership for his whore house. The green door squeaked as Joe pushed it open and walked in.

Every eye in the place was on Joe as he walked up to the bar. He didn't take it personally, he did the same thing when he played cards too. Joe's blue eyes searched the place for Jake and for anyone that might want to do him harm. A bar tender that Joe recognized from the last time came up to where he was standing. "What'll you have?" He asked.

"Two things." Joe said. "First I want a bottle of your best whiskey and second I want to know where Jake Benson is." The bartender eyed Joe as he placed the bottle on the bar.

Maple could hear the big door open to reveal four men standing there. One held a bucket of oatmeal, one held a lantern, one a box of bowls, and the last carried a gun. The slaves that had been there knew what the men were there for and crowded forward.

"Get back," the one with the gun said and all the slaves stopped dead in their tracks. A man in a white suit suddenly appeared in the doorway. The man handed each man money. "Thank you, Mr. Benson." Each man said as he was given money.

Maple watched as the man in the white suit was handed a little lantern. The man would hold his light above every slave's head as they were given a bowl. He would hook a finger under each slave's chin and raise their head and shine the light into their face.

"Well now what do we have here?" He asked as Maple's chin went up. Maple stared into the bluest eyes she had ever seen.

"Master I'ze Maple from Sams place. Master this is my mom." Maple said pointing to Meg beside her. Jake moved the lantern over just a little and saw Meg looking at him.

"Your name?" Jake asked.

"Meg, Master."

"Who is this Sam?" Jake asked the one holing the paper in his hand.

"Sam Sorrows." The man told him.

"Mark me down as a bidder." Jake told the man.

"Will do Mr. Benson." The man with the paper told him with a smile. "Is you going to be our new master?" Maple asked as she hugged her mom.

"We'll see." Jake told them as he went on down the line.

Maples eyes followed the man until all she could see was the light in the darkness. "He may not be the one to buy us." Meg said as she brushed her fingers through Maples hair.

"Did you see how he was looking at me?" Maple asked. "He will be my new master." She said. "That doesn't mean he will buy me." Meg said as she removed her fingers from Maples hair.

Sam had gone to the stock pens looking for Joe Carter. He got to the pens just as Jake and the men came out of the cell. "That's him, Mr. Benson. That's Sam Sorrows." The one with the papers said pointing to Sam. Sam walked up to the men going to ask if they knew where Joe Carter was.

"Mr. Sorrows, I'm Jake Benson and I'm very interested in some of your stock." Jake told Sam and stuck out his hand to shack Sams hand.

A big grin came to Sams face as he shook Jakes hand. "Which ones are you interested in?" Sam asked.

"The two white ones for sure and maybe a two more for my hotel." Jake said.

"Wished I had known about your hotel before me and my wife got a different one." Sam said.

A small laugh came from Jake as he through back his head. "I don't think your wife would like my place Mr.Sarrows. It's a brothel for the men who likes his women on the colored side."

"NO, I guess she would want to change." Sam said as he let go of Jakes' hand.

"Why don't we go to my place so we can talk in private." Jake said as he patted Sam on the back.

"That sounds good to me, you see I like a little dark meat every once in a while." Sam said as the two walked away.

Joe Carter poured what was left in the bottle into his glass and was just about to drink it when Jake and Sam walked in together. How could Sam know about the deal he was going to make before he made it?

"Well, if it ain't Joe Carter." Sam said as the two men came up to him.

"Sam, Jake." Joe said as he reached out to Jake to shake hands.

"I'd like to talk Joe but me and Sam Sorrows has some business to do so you have a bottle on the house." Jake said as he spoke to the bartender.

"Sure Mr. Benson." The bartender said as he placed a full bottle on the counter. Joe sat where he was and watched the two men go upstairs to Jakes office.

Sam was still gone when Mary finished her bath. Not having a slave servant to dry her off, Mary's thoughts went to Meg and how she must be scared to death by now. Both Meg and Maple had been good servants but she didn't want them on the plantation. The thought of Sam being with them was just too painful.

The thought of pain made Mary think of how much she would go through if she conceived. Mary had witnessed so many slaves having babies that she knew pain was involved. She had to admit when Maple told her that she was having a baby, Mary felt a little envious. She understood that Sam wanted a son and why. What worried her was the way Sam had sex with slaves that he fathered himself. Would he try that if he had a daughter? She didn't believe he would but she couldn't be sure. Mary shook off the thought and went back to dressing before

Sam came back.

Sam's blue eyes scanned Jakes office after the two of them entered it. Jake went behind the mahogany desk and sat down in the leather chair.

"Have a seat." Jake said pointing to the chair sitting across from him.

"This is a nice place you have here." Sam said as he waved his hand in the air.

"As you can see Mr.Sarrows, I like pretty things and you have a slave girl that I think is pretty. Now all we have to do is find out your price and determine if it too high." Jake said without stopping.

"Damn Mr. Benson you don't beat around the bush, do you?" Sam asked.

"No Mr. Sorrows I don't. So, give me your price." Jake said in a low voice.

Sam leaned back in his seat and scratched his chin. "Ten thousand for Maple, and two thousand a piece for the others."

Jake leaned back laughing. "You can't be serious. Now I'll tell you what I'll give, ten thousand for the six."

Sam rose from his chair and shook his head no without saying a word. "You best take my offer. It's better then what you'll get tomorrow on the block."

A smile came to Joe Carters face as he watched Sam come out of Jakes office. From the look on Sams face the two didn't make any kind of deal.

"Did you sell him the whole bunch?" Joe asked Sam as he walked up to him.

"No. The bastard wanted six slaves for the same price as I wanted for Maple." Sam said.

"Well Sam tomorrow you can come by and show him how much more you got for them." Joe said.

"By crackey your right Joe! I'll do that. I'll show him!" Sam said. "Carter, we need to talk. After the auction, we will not be needing your services." Sam said.

A very drunk Joe Carter came out of his chair. "Now you listen to me Sam, if you fire me the next place I'll be going is the sheriff's office and tell how you wanted me to kill your wife."

"Now don't get to hasty, Joe. This is all Mary's idea but I'm sure we can work around it."

"You just remember Sam. If I go down, you go with me." Joe said.

"Just stay out of Mary's sight." Sam told Joe as he went through the swinging doors. As soon as Sam had gotten out of sight, Joe headed up to Jakes office.

The night had been a long one for Maple and Meg. It had been so dark in the cell that you couldn't see your hand in front of you. Maple would no sooner drift off to sleep when a hair-raising scream would wake her again. It was just starting to get light outside when Maple fell asleep.

Her eyes popped open when she heard a sound that the men were back to feed them. Would the master in the white suit be with them again? Maples eyes strained to find him but couldn't. Once her eyes got use to the light what she saw struck fear in her.

There was only three men and they wasn't carrying food, they carried whips and guns. As the one with the whip got close enough she saw the face of Joe Carter. "Get to your feet girl. We are going for a walk." Joe said as he grabbed Maples arm and pulled her up.

Meg started to protest but when Joe drew back the whip all she could do was cry. Maple fell when she jerked her arm from Joes grip.

"On your feet or your ass, you are still going." Joe said as he grabbed Maples ankle and dragged her out the door.

Maple was being dragged like a log over the cobble stones and each one jarred her head when she hit it.

"What the hell do you think your doing?" Maple heard right before she saw a fist hit Joe up side the head. "Didn't you tell me she was with child?" Jake Benson asked pointing at Joe.

"Yes, but it's just one of Sam's suckers."

"Get to your feet girl!" Jake said as he stuck out his hand to help Maple up. "Come with me." Jake said as he turned and started walking, knowing Maple would follow. Maple stuck her chin in the air as she walked pass Joe laying on the ground. Maple kept walking as she looked back at the cell that held her mother.

Jake stood at a carriage that was driven by a large black man in a suit. He was holding the rains to a team of horses that were blacker then him. Maple felt like she was in a dream and couldn't wake up. Maples eyes were fixed on the floor not daring to look her new master in the face. Maple couldn't explain it but she felt safe with this strange white man.

Follow me was all he would say, then took the lead. Maple didn't know if it was because he seemed to know that if she tried to run she wouldn't get far or was it because he would be a good master. Maple decided that she could do a lot worse on the block.

When the team pulled up to a big building they were stopped. Jake lunged out of the carriage and didn't say a word. Maple was right behind him when he stopped at the foot of a stair case that went to the door that was three floors up. When Maple stepped through the door she saw that the room seemed to go forever with white columns running down the center of the building and at the very end there was a lion's head spitting water into a pool with colored fish. Jake didn't stop walking until he had reached his office.

"Do you understand that you don't belong to me yet?" Jake asked Maple shook her head no she didn't understand. "The reason you were brought here is because I wanted to talk to you before I bid on you." Jake said. "What's your name?"

"Maple master." she said looking at the floor.

"Maple you can look up if you want." Jake told Maple. Fear flashed over Maple when Jake wanted to know if she was going to have a baby. The only thing Maple could do was tell him the truth.

"Yes master. I'ze going to have a boy." Maple said in an excited voice.

Jake laughed then asked Maple, "How do you know it's a boy?"

"My mama told me. She knows how to cook the roots for medicine and how to birth and such. Master they say back on the plantation if your going to have a baby or is sick, you just call Meg and she will fix you right up. Master if you buy my mom she can do your doctoring."

"Is this a sneaky way to get me to buy your mom?" Jake asked.

Maples eyes went back to the floor as she shook her head yes.

"Your master is asking a lot of money for you so we'll buy you before thinking about your mom. Take off that rag you call a dress." Jake told Maple as he sat down in his chair. Maple hesitated for a second then pulled the burlap dress over her head and dropped it on the floor. Jake rose from his chair and came around the desk to Maple.

Maple had to fight the urge to try and hide her nude body. Jakes eyes went from top to bottom as he circled Maple stopping when he reached back in front of her. Jakes eyes never left Maples as he reached down and picked up the rough burlap dress Maple had been wearing.

"It's a crime that such beauty be hidden in a rag like this." He said handing Maple the dress. "I'll promise you Maple, If I buy you, you will never wear a rag like this again." Jake said as he sat back down.

"Master does you want me to put this rag back on?" Maple asked.

"I'm afraid so girl. You see if I prettied you up now it would just cost me more money at the auction." The thought of Jake not being her master frightened Maple. She realized she could end up with a master like Joe Carter or Sam. Maple made up her mind that she would do whatever she had to do to see that Master Benson would be her new Master. Meg was so pleased to see Maple come back through the cell house door.

Joe Carter stood in Jake Bensons office trying to think of a way he could tell Jake his offer. "Go ahead Joe, tell me what you came here to say. I have an auction to go to." Jake told Joe.

"I wanted to tell you, if you really wanted Maple he could get her for him for a thousand dollars." Joe said.

"Carter you are as low as a man can get. As far as I'm concerned any man that would steal from his employer might come in handy someday but today isn't it." Jake said as he showed Joe the door.

Jake was surprised to see Sam Sorrows at one of his poker tables as he reached the bottom of the stairs. Jake walked over and told the dealer to take a break and he would fill in for him.

"You better keep your eye on that one." He told Jake pointing toward Sam. "He's down Five thousand already."

Jake understood what the dealer was talking about after a few hands with Sam.

He was so sure that the next hand would be his that he would bid a hundred at a time. Jake was surprised and pleased at the same time when Sam asked the hundred dollar limit be lifted.

"This is getting to steep for me." the other two players said as they rose to leave.

Sam searched his pockets for more money but found none. Sam had bet two thousand and Jake had raised him five.

"I don't have any more money with me but I can pay you after the sale." Sam said.

"You know the rules Sam. If you can't cover the bet you lose." Jake reminded Sam.

"Now just wait there Benson. I've got something you may want." Sam said as his hand went to a vest pocket and retrieved the deeds to the slaves he had brought with him. "This is the deed to Maple." Sam said as he placed the papers on the stack of chips.

"Very well. What do you have?" Jake asked Sam.

"I have four aces." Sam said with a grin and threw his cards on the table.

"That won't beat a straight flush in hearts." Jake told Sam as he raked in the deed and chips.

"Let's play one more hand." Sam said holing the rest of the deeds out for Jake to see.

"I'm afraid not. I've got an auction to go to. Maybe we could play some more after the auction is over. Jake rose from the table and motioned for the dealer to come back to the table.

Sam just sat trying to think of a what he was going to tell Mary about Maple.

The women were lined up in a straight line and marched one at a time to the block. Both Meg and Maple watched as the women in front of them were taken to the block. Two of the girls were sick as they took them to the block. Maple noticed that the men didn't pay as much for the sick girls as they did for the healthy ones. Maple turned to Meg.

"Do as I do mom. Just watch me and do it." Maple said as she was taken to the block. It wasn't hard for Maple to make herself sick by putting her fingers in her throat. The hot noon sun had already caused her white body to sweat. Maple fell to her knees on the platform and began puking.

The sound of grounds told Maple that she was getting the response she was looking for. Maple was in the middle of her act when she saw Master Benson run to the front of the men. Fear flashed through Maple until she saw a smile on his face.

"This slave is not for sale." Jake said holding up the deed.

"Get that sick bitch out of here." Came a voice from the crowd.

Joe Carter was outraged when he saw Jake with the deed to Maple. Joe watched as Meg was brought to the block next.

"Please Master she be a good baby doctor." Maple begged. Jake watched as Meg was striped and examined. She was good enough for his place anyway so Jake decided to bid on Meg, "one thousand." Jake said. By the time the bid got back to Jake the bid was up to four thousand. It would take two thousand customers to pay for her, Jake thought. Jake was about to quit bidding until he looked at Maple. One more bid he thought as he yelled five to an astonished crowd. After the hammer had fallen three times, Meg was allowed to dress and join her daughter.

"Thank you master." Meg said as Maple started to say something. Jake held up one of his fiThngers, "Don't ask me to buy anyone else." Jake said.

"No master I'z won't." Maple said turning her eyes to the ground. "Follow me." Jake said leading the way through the crowd.

Maple grabbed Megs hand and waited until Jakes back was to her before she allowed a big grin to cover her face.

"Why ain't you down at the auction?" Mary asked.

"I had Carter stay there to keep an eye on things for us before I tell him he's fired." Sam said as he took Mary into his arms.

Mary thought of pushing Sam away but it would cause a fight and Sam was rough enough at sex as it was.

Sam was expecting Mary to push him off her and when she didn't Sam undid the first button on Mary's dress. It surprised Mary when Sam was more gentle with her now then he was on their wedding night.

Mary hated to admit it but after it was all over she had enjoyed it. She knew it was all over when Sam yelled "Mary our son is here!" As Mary laid in the bath, she was feeling good about her plan to take over the Shady Sorrows and with Joe Carter out of the way. Sam will have to come to her for help the very first time a problem came up. As soon as I get control I'll purge the Shady Sorrows of its nigger off spring, she could tell you.

"That reminds me, I wonder how much he got for Meg and Maple? I'll have to ask Sam."

Meg and Maple were led to the back door of a three-story building on bourbon street. Jake used his key to let them inside. Both Meg and Maple gave a gasp when they stepped inside.

The whole floor was covered in bright red carpet and long red drapes hung from each window. On a mantel above the fireplace sat three toy ships. Jake walked over to a table and picked up a tiny bell and rang it. Turning to Meg and Maple, "You can take off them rags" he said pointing at Maples dress.

"Yes Master." Maple said reaching down and pulling the burlap dress over her head.

Jake saw that Meg was frightened so he went to her. "I'm not going to hurt you. I'm just giving you two a bath before you get a clean dress."

Meg looked into Jakes eyes and knew she had nothing to fear from this master. As the burlap dress left contact with her skin did Meg feel free for the first time. A door came open and a woman the size of Carter came through it.

"Well Jake you brought me a couple of pretty ones this time." The large woman said.

Goose bumps came to Maples legs and arms when Jake walked over to her and placed his hand on Maples stomach. "Master it wasn't her fault she was forced to." Meg said. "You can let it be born then sell it if you want."

"You don't talk to your Master unless he tells you, do you understand?" Jake said angrily.

"I'z sorry Master!" Meg said as her eyes returned to the floor.

"You want me to teach them some manners?" The two-hundred-pound red headed woman asked.

"No Eva. They are not for you. I just want them washed and some dresses put on them."

"But Jake don't you know how much money we can make with these two?" Eva asked.

"No Eva I have plans for these two myself. Now be sweet and clean them up for me."

"Your the boss but I see a lot of money in them." Eva said.

I may give you the older one later on. "Jake told her as Eva lead the two women out.

The pretty slave girl carries the Benson heir in her. The heir he could no longer produce. His doctor told him he was dying of cancer and since the cancer was attacking his reproductive system he could no longer get an heir the normal way.

"Fine job." Sam said to each one of the overseers as he paid him some money and a handshake. Carter I want you to move your things into the old plantation house and stay out of Mary's sight." Sam told him.

"Sam you got the back bone of a worm." Joe said as he took his money.

"Where are the others?" Mary asked as she took her seat on the covered wagon beside Sam.

"I sent them on ahead. We will catch up with them later on." Sam said as he flicked the reins lightly over the horse's rear to make them walk.

"Oh, by the way. How much did Meg and Maple bring?" Mary asked.

Sam studied her before he answered. "Five thousand is all." He told her.

"Why so little? I thought that Meg would have brought that by herself." Mary said.

"That Maple acted like she was sick so she didn't bring as good as we thought." Sam said.

"Who bought her?" Mary asked.

"I sold her and Meg to a whore house on bourbon street." Sam told Mary.

Sam was surprised to hear the little giggle that came from Mary.

"And what did Joe Carter say when you let him go?" Mary asked.

Sam turned his head and looked to the woods as he lied to her. "OH he cussed and threatened to beat my ass but he took the money and left."

"Well I'm glad the bastard is gone." Mary said.

It was getting late when Sam and Mary reached sight of the overseers and slave camp. Sam stopped his wagon and set up his camp just in sight of the other camp sight.

"Why are you not going over there?" Mary asked knowing all the time why Sam stopped here.

The thick wooden door fell off its hinges when Joe Carter kicked it with his boot. A cloud of dust almost filled the room as Joe stepped in. Sam better pay me extra for this, he said in a low voice. The house had been built on the plantation and after the fire in one of the bedrooms the second house was built. I'll get me a few of them wenches to clean up the place, and this won't be half bad. Now I can do anything I want and Sam won't do anything about it." Joe said out loud. "All I have to do is tell him that I'm going to see Mary and his goose is cooked."

"Through them rags into that box and get into the water." Eva told Maple and Meg as they entered a room with a large tub. "Come on, get on with it." Eva said with aggravation in her voice when Meg and Maple just stood and stared at the tub like it was some kind of beast.

As Maple and Meg sat down in the water Eva walked over to a door and called for Lizzy, a light skinned slave. Rose was darker in color but the prettiest of the two Maple thought.

After Meg and Maple was seated Rose and Lizzy each picked up a rag and began washing them both. When Rose finished Maple, she handed her the washcloth and told her to wash herself just like she had done.

Maple took the soapy rag and began washing. Meg didn't wait for Lizzy to finish before she grabbed the rag from Lizzy's hand.

"You can wash yourself if you want to but I'm going to stand right here and see that you do it right." Lizzy told her.

The water seemed hot to Maple but it was so clean that maple could see the bottom of the tub. No one else had ever used it before.

Jake was playing cards when Joe Carter came into the room and stood at the bar. "I'm out." Jake told the men at the table as he threw his cards onto the table. "I thought you had left with Sorrows." Jake said as he came and stood beside Joe.

"I decided to stay over for a few days and enjoy the fruit of my labor." Joe laughed.

"I'm glad to hear it Joe because the longer you stay the richer I get." Jake said as he motioned for the bartender to give Joe a free one.

Joe looked around to see who was close enough to hear what he was saying, but decided that no one was. "I know a way to make me rich and you richer." Joe said not taking his eyes off Jake.

"I've never known a man who didn't want to be richer then he was." Jake said staring back at Joe.

"The truth is that Sam fired me and now I'm going to become a slave peddler." Joe said as he drank down his free drink.

"How is you getting fired going to make me richer?" Jake asked.

"It's simple Jake. I'm going to travel all over buying slaves and you can have first pick at a low price."

"I'll tell you what Joe. You get them here and I'll buy them from you." Jake said as he walked away.

"Follow me." Eva told Meg and Maple then began walking to a room full of clothes.

Of all the clothes hanging in the room Maples eyes locked on a white dress with yellow flowers. "Oh mama, was we sold into slavery or heaven?" Maple asked as she took the dress off the hanger.

Megs eyes scanned the room, all these clothes couldn't belong to this one woman. Like a slap in the face, Meg knew what they were sold into. Tears filled Megs eyes as she told Maple that the hell they had been sold into was no heaven.

"What did you think Master Benson bought you so he could marry you?" Eva asked.

"No Ms. Eva. I never think that." Meg said looking at the floor.

Maple heard what Eva was saying and realized that she would have to pay for her keep. The fear that all men were like Master Carter came back to Maple. Maples concentration broken as Jake entered the room. He could never be that bad, she told herself as she stood holding the flowered dress.

A smile tugged at Jake's mouth but he was able to stop it before it became obvious. "Put it on if that's the one you like Maple, and let me see how you look in it." Jake said.

With a smile Maple pulled the dress over her head then put her arms through the sleeves.

"Girl don't you know to put your arms in first?" Eva said as she helped Maple get her arms through the sleeves. Maples finger tips were touching the finest china silk money could buy.

"Master does I get to keep this dress?" Maple asked as her hands felt the smooth silk.

"Yes, you get to keep it as long as it fits." Jake had to admit Maple looked beautiful in that dress. He stood and watched as Maple pulled her long black hair up through the collar. Jakes eyes went to Maples belly that pushed on the silk dress.

Meg had picked a plain black dress made of cotton and after

wearing burlap for so long the cotton lay softly on her skin. Maybe Maple had been right, this was heaven and not the hell she expected. Meg looked at the way Master Jake was looking at Maple and she was frightened.

It had been three months since Mary and Sam had gotten back from New Orleans. Mary had not gotten pregnant while she was there. Mary couldn't decide if it made her happy or not. The thought of all the slave girls she had helped give birth and died, scarred her.

But she was turning thirty-one next week and her body reminded her that time for a child bearing was running out. She wanted a baby but was afraid to have one. "I'll bet that Maple was about to drop that Joe Carter sucker by now." If the baby had belonged to Sam, she would have kept the baby and raised it as her own. "That's right Mary. Sam would go for that." She said out loud. The only way she can please him was to have a baby herself.

It had to be her fault for not having a baby because Sam was getting slave girls pregnant all the time so it couldn't be him. A tear ran down her cheek. Face it Mary you are to be childless. Sam's and Mary's sex life had gone pretty good for two months after they got back but for the last month Sam was back with his slaves.

Sam sat in his high back chair with the soft cushions drinking a glass of moonshine as Easter entered the room.

"What do you want?" Sam asked in a hard voice.

"Master Sam, Miss Mary say for me to tell you that your food is getting cold." Easter said.

"Where is Otis?" Sam asked.

"You sent him up to fix you a bath, master." Easter said.

"Oh yeah." Sam said as he rose from his seat. He was almost to his feet when Sam started to fall backwards. Easter reached out purely by instinct and grabbed Sam's arm and caught him.

Before Easter knew what was happening the arm she had grabbed had wrapped around her waist. "Easter help me up to the tub and I'll let you wash me instead of Otis."

"Master Sam, I sure would like to do that, but Miss Mary has some more chores so I best be getting back to her." Easter told Sam.

"I don't give a damn what Miss Mary wants. I'm the king of this castle." Sam roared.

"Yes Master! Easter just don't want Miss Mary to think I was doodling."

"Well we can't have Miss Mary thinking like that so you help me to the top of the stairs. Then you can go on with your work." Sam told Easter as his arm went around her neck. As soon as Sam and Easter reached the top of the stairs and Sam removed his arm from around Easter's neck she headed down the stairs.

She had put up with his sexual advances before but never here in the big house. Miss Mary was the power over the house servants and until now even Master Sam knew it. Easter knew that with Meg and Maple gone she had no one to help with keeping Master Sam's urges satisfied. Mary looked up as Easter entered the dining room.

"Well did you find him?' Mary asked.

"Yes mam. He say he's coming soon as he takes his bath." Easter said.

"Is he drunk?" Mary asked.

"Yes mam." Easter said looking at the floor.

"You can go help Minnie in the kitchen." I'll wait here a while longer.

"Mary said. Easter left the room without taking her eyes off the floor. She knew that she had to get away from Miss Mary before she asks her if Master Sam had made a pass at her.

Mary was just getting ready to leave when Sam and Otis entered the room. Otis was right behind Sam as if holding him up to keep him from falling. "Otis you go see if them boys packed that bath water out." Sam said as Otis pulled out his chair. As soon as Otis left Mary turned to Sam.

"Sam I think we have someone stealing our slaves."

"What gives you that idea?" Sam asked.

"Well it's been three months since we got back from New Orleans and we have had three slaves run off." Mary said sitting back in her chair.

"I know we had three runners but that don't mean someone is stealing from us!" Sam shouted.

"I know that we never had more than two to try and run in a year and now we are losing one a month." Mary shouted back as she rose from the table.

"Now don't get mad at me. It must be the head overseers' fault, he just not as good at keeping an eye on the niggers as Carter was." Sam said motioning for Mary to sit back down.

"Well he is just going to get better or he will have to go." Mary said as she sat back down.

Maple sat up in bed holding a very hungry boy to her breast. The baby didn't open his eyes very often but when he did it revealed the bluest eye's Meg had ever seen. Maple tried to press down on her breast so the boy could breathe while he sucked.

The way he pushed his nose into her he couldn't catch his breath through his nose. "He's so pretty." Meg said as she rubbed the back of her fingers over the boys face.

Jake entered the room with his eyes locked on the baby. "Which is it a boy or girl?"

"Oh, he is being a little jackass." Maple said. Jake didn't try to hide his smile.

"That's it." He said as he sat down on the bed.

"That's what?" Maple asked knowing she had no power to stop whatever it was.

"That's going to be his name, Jack Benson." Jake said as his hands held his son for the first time. Maple liked the name she was afraid the Master was going to give him a nigger name like Otis or something like that. Yes, Jack pleased her.

"Are you sure Dr. Fox?" Mary asked.

"Yes Mrs. Sorrows I'm sure you are at least four months. You should have come in earlier." Fox said as he took Mary's feet from the sturips.

"Well doctor I thought I was missing because of other things."

"Mary you know as well as I do that you have been afraid of getting pregnant."

"Sam can't know about this now doc."

"You won't be able to keep it from him for long if he doesn't already know."

"Promise me doctor that you won't tell him." Mary asked in a louder tone. "Ok Mary but Sam can tell a pregnant woman before I can just by the way she looks. You know that."

"I'll tell him as soon as he asks. I promise." Mary told Fox as she left his office. Mary couldn't believe she was finally with child. It seemed like only yesterday when Sam had taken her to New Orleans to get her to get her this way.

It was hard to believe it had been fifteen years. Later that night Mary's heart jumped to her throat when Sam asked her what the doctor had told her. Mary could tell how much it hurt Sam when she told him she was going through the change. He said that a woman my age was taking a risk having a baby. Sam's face light up as he realized what Mary was saying.

It had been ten hours from the time Mary's water broke and doctor Fox had been found and brought there.

"Well doc, how long before she has it?" Sam asked when Fox finished his examination.

"This is her first Sam. It's going to take her a while, you know that." The grandfather clock down stairs rang out ten. "Sam you go down stairs and have a drink. Me and Easter can take care of Mary and the baby seems to be in good health."

"Well, okay but I'll be back in a few minutes." Sam said. Old doc Fox smiled because he knew that once Sam started turning up that jug he would pass out before he came back.

Mary cried out in pain as doctor Fox came back in the room. "Now Mary it's going to be a while longer and crying out loud won't make it any sooner."

"I'll cry as loud as I want." Mary said as the contraction stopped.

Easter wiped the sweat from Mary's head with a wet cloth. Mary was in labor for another four hours before the baby girl finally came. The sun was just peeping over the hills as doctor Fox slapped the baby on her bottom to make her cry. Mary named her Dawn.

Right after Jack turned three was the last time Maple had talked to her mother and that was fifteen years ago. Master Jake had treated her good because little Jack didn't know who his mother was. If it wasn't for that she had no dought that Master Jake would have her in the same place Meg was sent to.

Maple smiled as she thought of how her son had grown to be a fine man. He was only eighteen but he run most of Master Jakes business already. It thrilled her to watch her son stand up to any man black or white. Not for a minute letting Jack know you couldn't tell just by looking at Jack that he had a drop of her blood in him.

There was one thing that she could say for Master Jake. He truly loved that boy as if it was his blood in his veins. Master Jake had been in bed for two months so weak he couldn't get out of it. Maple had been surprised that Master Jake had lasted this long. Jake was asleep now so Maple was going to find Jack. The person she found standing in Jacks office turned her blood to ice. Joe Carter sat in a chair in front of the desk.

"Well Mr. Benson, me and your father had a little business that was let's say was paid in cash and he owes me five thousand." Joe Carter was saying.

"What I'm saying Mr. Carter is I don't know you and don't want to know you. Until my father comes back, I'm in charge and I'm not giving you a dime." Jack said rising from his chair.

Joe Carter was no fool he could tell that Jake Benson was this boy's father. "I will talk to my father then get back to you Mr. Carter." Jack was saying as he showed Joe to the door.

Maple hid in another room until Master Carter had gone before she finished her trip to see her son. Jack was going through some papers when Maple entered the room. That was another thing Master Jake had done for her son, he sent him to one of the best schools. Why there wasn't a thing Jack couldn't read. Maple longed to tell Jack she was his mother but she would not risk being put on the block.

"How is my father Maple?" Jack asked.

"He is asleep now Master Jack. He will sleep for a while." Maple said.

"You know Maple, you have been like a mother to me since my real mother died in child birth." Jack said.

"Now Master Jack, it's been fun playing mother to you." Maple said.

"My father was sure lucky the day he bought you." Jack said looking at Maple's eyes that looked at the floor.

"Maple you don't have to look at the floor when you talk to me. Do you need to talk to me about something or is this a social visit?" Jack asked.

Without looking up, Maple found the courage to ask Jack about her future. "Master Jack what is to happen to me if something happens to Master Jake?"

Jack fell back in his chair laughing. "Are you thinking about going somewhere Maple?" Jack asked when he stopped laughing.

"Oh no Master Jack. I don't want to go nowhere. I'm happy right here with you. Please don't sell Maple if Master Jake goes." Maple cried with real fear in her voice. There was no dought that Maple was frightened. Jack couldn't understand what Maple was afraid of.

"I'll never sell you Maple, you are the only mother I have ever known. So tell me what is frightening you so much." Jack asked as he came around the desk to Maple.

"I was thinking about my mother and how she was sold off years ago." "As long as I'm around you won't be sold." Jack assured Maple as he placed his arm around her neck and hugged her.

"Now I've got work to do. So go on with your cleaning." Jack told Maple as he showed her the door. As Jack looked at the people downstairs he saw Joe Carter at the bar.

There was something about the man Jack didn't like besides claiming he owed him money.

"Come and tell me as soon as father is awake." Jack told Maple before she left.

Eva caught Jack as he was going back to his desk. "We have a problem Jack." Eva said as she flopped down in a chair.

"What is it this time Eva? One of your girls get knocked?" Jack asked. "No Jack we have a real problem one of the customers is giving the girls vd." Eva said.

"Which customer is it?" Jack asked with real alarm.

"That's the problem. We don't know but every which one it is he done infected three of our girls."

That's just the ones we know about. Jack told Eva as he started going through the records looking for a common denominator.

Cotton was five years old on that rainy day the twins were born. He had no idea what was bringing in all these people to his and his mother's cabin but he could feel the excitement. All of the sudden he heard a cry from his mother and then from old Minnie, who worked in the kitchen, there appeared a little baby crying at the top of her lungs.

Cotton didn't know what kind of magic the old woman had, but he had seen it for himself. The second cry from his mother brought Cotton out of his seat to his feet. And just like before there appeared another crying baby.

"Don't you make my mamma cry no more!" Cotton said standing his ground at three feet. Cottons bluff was good until he saw Minnie's head come up again and this time her eyes were locked on Cotton.

"And just what are you going to do about it Cotton?" Minnie asked.

"Miss Minnie, I can't get the bleeding to stop." Cotton heard another voice say.

"Cotton come here." He heard his mother saying.

"Easter you should save your energy." Minnie was saying as he approached the bed.

Both babies crying brought Cottons attention to them laying at the foot of the bed.

"Cotton, come here baby, mama got something to tell you." Easter put her arm around Cottons back and hugged him "You may have to go stay with someone else after today."

"You now have two sisters to take care of. I know I'm asking a lot from you at your age but I've run out of time." Another cry of pain brought Minnie in between Cotton and his mother.

Cotton went back to the corner and sat down. He wasn't there long before Minnie ordered one of the other women to take him out of there. May was the girl Master Sam had put in Megs old cabin. It was raining hard as May pushed Cotton through the door of the dark cabin.

Cotton stood frozen in the darkness until May lite a candle. May could hear snickering of a horse so she blew the candle back out.

"May why did you blow out the light?" Cotton asked.

"I think your pappy's out there and if he sees my light he'll be in here pestering me."

Minnie was putting cover over Easters body when Master Sam walked in.

"I'm sorry Master Sam but Easter's gone. She left you two girls before she left." Minnie said with tears in her eyes and pointed to the foot of the bed. Sam walked to the side of the bed and pulled back the cover.

"I can tell you one thing old girl, I'm going to have the carpenters build you a wood coffin." Sam said before putting back the cover over Easters face. Sam turned to Minnie. "She told me that she had a name picked out for a girl. Did she tell you what it was?" Sam asked.

"Yes, she did. She wanted to name her Vera but she didn't know there were two Master." Sam moved to the foot of the bed and picked up one of the crying babies.

"This one I'll call Vera and that one Cara." Sam said pointing at the other baby. "Where's the boy?" Sam asked as he placed the baby on the bed. The sound of the door being pushed open took every one's eyes to it.

"How is she?" Mary asked as she came through the door. As soon as Mary's eyes got use to the light she saw Easters covered body and the twin girls.

"Oh my God!" Mary said putting her hand to her mouth.

"She lived long enough to have these." Sam said pointing at the twins. "There just as white as Cotton was." Mary said as she picked one of the babies up in her arms and cradled it. Marys breast hung close to the baby's mouth and before Mary knew it she was trying to suck on Mary.

It had been three years since Dawn nursed at her breast and Mary remembered how much she liked it.

"This child is hungry." Mary said as she looked at Easters dead body. "Uncover her breast." Mary ordered Minnie. Mary placed the baby she was holding down on Easters chest then placed the nipple of Easters swollen breast in the babies mouth. The baby stopped crying and eagerly sucked at the milk that was held in the swollen breast. After placing the other twin so it could suck the other breast Mary sent Minnie to find a wet nurse for the babies.

"And when you find her bring her to the big house."

"What do you mean, bring her to the big house?" Sam asked. "Do you mean to raise these babies?"

"No but until we decide what to do with them. They will stay in one of the extra rooms."

Dawn was almost four the morning she awoke and climbed out of bed where she and her mother slept. A pretty butterfly that was basking in the first sun rays of morning caught Dawns eye. Just before reaching it, the butterfly took flight out into the hall.

Dawn looked at her mother's sleeping figure before she followed the butterfly. At the end of the hall there was an open door and the sound coming out of it excited Dawn. Dawn had to see what was making those sounds. She peeked around the open door and the thing she saw laying on the bed caused Dawns mouth to fly open. Mommy had gotten her a live doll that made sounds.

"What you looking at?" The wet nurse asked with a laugh. Dawn hadn't noticed the black woman holding another doll to her breast. "It's alright child come in. I'm just feeding the babies." Hazel said motioning for Dawn to come to her.

Dawn moved slowly until she was within arm's length of her before she stopped. Dawn couldn't believe what she was seeing, there was two live dolls. Reaching out with her finger, Dawn poked the babies belly. A smile came to Dawns face when she realized that this wasn't a dream.

"What you doing in here little miss?" Dawn heard a familiar voice ask from behind her.

"I want to play with the dolls." Dawn said as she turned to Otis.

"What dolls?" Otis asked as he knelt beside Dawn.

"That one and that one." Dawn said pointing at the babies.

"Those ain't dolls Miss Dawn, them real babies." Otis tried to explain. "Them people like me and you only smaller." Otis said as he took Dawns hand and lead her out.

"No!" Dawn said as she jerked her hand free from Otis' grip. "I want to play with the dolls"

The girl that was to be keeping an eye on Dawn appeared in the doorway. "Where have you been that you couldn't see a child run through the house unattended?" Otis' voice barked at the girl.

"I'm sorry Otis. I've been down in the kitchen with Minnie." The girl said as she took a hold of Dawns arm.

"Miss Dawn you come with me and I'll play dolls with you." The thirteen-year-old girl said pulling on Dawns arm with more force then Otis liked.

"Let go of that child's arm." Otis said as he stood up.

"I'm going to tell my mommy!" Dawn said as she ran out the door crying for her mother. "Mommy, mommy!" Dawn was saying as she ran through the door and jumped on to the bed.

"What is it Dawn?" Mary asked as she struggled to get awake.

"Otis won't let me play with them dolls you bring me." Dawn said as she climbed into her mother's arms. Mary tried to think of what dolls her daughter was talking about when the slave girl came into the room.

"What is going on here?" Mary asked when Otis appeared next in her bedroom doorway.

"I'm sorry Miss Mary but this girl left Miss Dawn alone and she went to the room with the babies and she thinks their dolls." Otis said. It even surprised Dawn when her mother started laughing at their troubles.

"Mommy will take you to see the babies as soon as all these people get out of my room so I can get dressed. And Otis you are over the house slaves so you deal with her." Miss Mary said pointing at the girl that followed him out. This had been the second girl that Miss Mary had tried since Easter stopped working.

Miss Mary had told him to find her a good girl like Maple was. Otis told miss Mary that he was trying his best but he hadn't found her yet.

Otis waited until the girl was in the hall before he stopped her. "You were supposed to be watching that child and you were down in the kitchen. That won't happen anymore I can assure you." Otis said angerly. "You get whatever you own and get out of here." The girl started crying and started to explain but Otis pointed towards the outside said "Out!" as he turned and left the girl crying to herself.

The girl had gone by the time Dawn and Mary came out to see the twins. The wet nurse was just laying the last sleeping baby down on the bed as Miss Mary and Miss Dawn came in.

"They is both feed Miss Mary." Lizzy said as she moved aside for Mary. "You must be that Miss Dawn I been hearing about." Lizzy told Dawn as she cupped Dawns chin.

"Can I play with your dolls?" Dawn asked.

"Well Miss Dawn, my dolls are asleep now but if you come back in a while. I'll let you play with one while I feed the other." Liz said with a smile.

"Can I mom?" Dawn asked with excitement.

Mary liked the way the woman handled this problem. Mary found her new house servant. Dawn spent every spare minute playing with her dolls as she now called the twins. Mary was starting to worry because Dawn wanted to spend time with them niggers instead of with her. Then on the other hand it gave Mary more time to check on the missing slaves she had been told about.

Mary called for Otis so she could find out where Sam had gone. "Yes Miss Mary, he told me he was going up to the old house where Master Carter lives." Sam must have went to help find the runners. Mary thought as she ordered Otis to have a horse saddled.

Sam went out to see Joe Carter about getting rid of Mary but for good. "Of course, you'll have to make it look like an accident." Sam was saying to Joe, who sat in a chair with a sawed off shot gun laying in his lap.

"Tell me again just what's in it for me." Joe asked. Joe Carter didn't like the way Sam looked away from him before he answered.

"Well when Mary is no longer with us I'll give you ten percent of each year's profit." Joe rubbed his finger over the shot gun like he was petting a dog. If Sam was serious and could be trusted that wasn't a bad offer.

Mary had decided to cross over the creek bed and take the short cut to the old house when she met Sam and Joe Carter coming towards her.

"Mary, what are you doing here?" Sam asked as he stopped his horse.

"I thought I would come help you find them runners."Mary said without taking her eyes off Joe.

"Oh that. Joe found where the crocks got them." Sam said.

"Sam are you crazy or what? Joe Carter is the crock feeder around here!" Mary said.

"Why you bitch!" Joe yelled as he hit Mary's horse. on its nose with a whip. The horse reared in the air and since Mary was ridding side saddle she was tossed high in the air. Mary hit the rocks with a thump. Her head found the largest rock in the creek bed and hit it hard.

"My God! Look what you done." Sam said in shock. I done just what you wanted Sam so I'll be expecting my money the next sale. "Joe Carter said with unblinking eyes.

"What are you talking about Carter? I'm going to the sheriff now!"

Sam said.

"You do that Sam and your neck will get stretched right along with mine. Or have you forgotten who you hired to do this?" Joe asked.

Dawn was playing with her dolls when Sam came and picked her up. "No daddy I want to play some more." Dawn cried. Minnie was standing behind him wiping tears from her eyes. Dawn started crying and yelling at Minnie that she couldn't have her dolls back.

"No, no sweet heart she's not here for your dolls." Sam paused before going on, "It's your mother, she's had an accident sweetheart. Your mother won't be with us no longer. Dawn had no idea what her pa was saying just as long as that voo doo women knew who's dolls they were.

"Either she doesn't understand or she don't give a damn. Sam said as he handed Dawn to Minnie.

"NO pa, no!" Dawn cried slapping at Minnie.

"Come to me child." Liz said reaching out to Dawn. With no hesitation Dawn went into Lizzy's arms.

"Master Sam this child is scared to death of Minnie."

"What is it sweetie that makes you so afraid of Minnie?" Sam asked as he gave Dawn a hug.

"Lucy told her that she was a magic woman, a voo doo queen. Lucy was the slave Otis had fired for leaving Dawn alone."

"I'll have that bitch whipped before she was sold. Minnie go on back to the kitchen and Liz will watch over Dawn while I suffer my grief." Sam told Minnie. "Will you stay with Liz?" Sam asked Dawn.

"It's about feeding time." Liz said pointing at the twins.

Jack was now twenty-seven years old and the sole owner of the gambling and the whore houses. If you had money he would play against you but it had to be no limit or Jack wouldn't play. When Jack saw Joe Carter sitting at a card table with another man that Jack knew to be Sam Sorrows. The man everyone knew as an easy mark.

www.ingramcontent.com/pod-product-compliance
Lightning Source LLC
Chambersburg PA
CBHW031228120626
46545CB00003B/1031